Baptism and Beyond

Preparing for Baptism and Nurturing Your Child's Spirituality

Kathy Coffey

Kathy Coffey

Living the Good News
   a division of Church Publishing Incorporated
600 Grant Street, Suite 400
Denver, CO 80203

Imprimatur: † Most Reverend Charles J. Chaput, O.F.M. Cap.
Archbishop of Denver
June 21, 2000

The *imprimatur* is an official declaration that a book or pamphlet is free from doctrinal and
moral error. No implication is contained therein that those who have granted the *imprimatur* agree
with the contents, opinions or statements expressed.

Living the Good News
    a division of Church Publishing Incorporated
Editorial Offices:
600 Grant Street, Suite 400
Denver, CO 80203

Cover Design: Tom Castanzo
Cover Illustration: Martha Doty
Page Design and Art Direction: Sue MacStravic
Photography and Photo Manipulation: Regan MacStravic
    with additional photos by Sara Francis (pp. 6, 43, 52, 53, 61, 89, 92, 93, 95, 101, 104, 113)
    and Steve Skjold (pp. 1, 19, 20, 34, 44, 57, 65, 67, 102, 105, 152, 158)

Illustrations: Julie Durrell
Craft Diagrams: Anne Kosel
Project Editor: Steve Mueller

ISBN 978-1889108-72-8
ISBN 1-889108-72-3

Contents

Background

If you are the parent of a newborn or a young child, you probably feel overwhelmed: exhausted from sleepless nights, unsure how the newest family member will change your life, wanting desperately to be a good parent but wondering where to begin. The next twenty or so years loom like a long time ahead, too hard to imagine. If you're like other new parents, you may feel that this tiny infant, sweet and vulnerable, has been placed trustingly in your arms—and you don't have a clue what to do!

Much of the parental task in the early years is physical—many parents feel that just keeping baby clean and fed demands most of their energy. The routine of diapers, laundry, bathing and feeding consumes most of their time. When someone suggests seeing to the child's spiritual needs too, it seems like one more pressure on an already full agenda.

But what people are pointing to is not another burden, but an opportunity, a potential you'll never have again. The practices you establish now in your home will soon carry the weight of tradition, or "we've always done it this way." Take it on trust; even a balky two-year-old is more open to parental modeling and suggestions than a sixteen-year-old will ever be. Now is the time when, even unconsciously, you have an enormous influence on your growing child.

Many parents want to do the perfect job of parenting and have the perfect child. So it's dismaying to meet parents who honestly thought they did everything right, and still have major problems with their teenaged and young adult children. But the good news is that if your family has a spiritual core and base, God will be with you in the mistakes as well as the joys. If you're human, you'll fail plenty of times. But in God's eyes, all is forgiven; nothing is ever lost. The grace of baptism carries us through nights of croup and days of diapers.

While your child's first communion may seem like a long way off, this book looks forward to that day. The time between baptism and first eucharist is precious and irreplaceable. During the next few years, your child's basic religious outlook is being formed. You have the opportunity to give your child what the adage calls "roots and wings"—both deep grounding in an abiding faith and high ideals that invite your child to soar and become more than anyone, even the proudest parent, thought possible.

Use this resource not only to record your child's milestones as you would in a baby book, but to record your own process of parenting, as you grow into the role. Respond to the questions because they will prompt you to think at a level beyond pressing surface needs. You may think that the demands of your baby exhaust you, but this time is too important to treat superficially. Record it as a treasure you wish to preserve now and cherish in years to come. Look on it as a keepsake for your child— or yourself!

Part 1
The Symbols and Scriptures of Baptism

Awed by the crashing power of the
tremendous waves, ...[children] do something that we may ourselves have done....
They turn their backs "on what was too
awesome" and dig a hole.

Chapter 1

From Birth to the Baptismal Font

When you hold your child in your arms, what do you feel?

Many parents would answer that they feel a combination of emotions they have never have felt before: love, concern, vulnerability, joy, wonder, fear, hope, pride—all mingled together. Our confusion is almost impossible to describe. Even in speaking with a spouse, parent or close friend, we grope for words and bumble through explanations that don't quite capture reality.

For centuries, Christian parents have known this same puzzlement. We wobble on a new threshold. Somehow we know that this tiny creature has completely changed our lives and that we are experiencing the sacred in a new way. Our powerful emotions may be due to the fact that this child is such a powerful reminder of God in our lives. The love we feel for a child opens a window, gives us a glimmer, a hint of knowing how much God loves us. We may feel overwhelmed by it or think this is the greatest force we have ever encountered in our lives, yet it is only a fraction of God's love for us.

We feel awed because suddenly, we are in the presence of the creator. "As little as we can explicitly name...the experience of love...how much less can we name fully the real presence of God in our midst."[1] No one who

takes seriously their own limitations could argue that they alone were responsible for this marvelous small person, who in six or eight or ten pounds is equipped with finer brain, hearing, vision, and muscular system than the best engineer could ever have designed. Furthermore, something in that infant surpasses anything any human being could ever create—a transcendence, a uniqueness, what some might call an eternal soul.

Perhaps because of our awe and puzzlement around the time of birth or adoption, we reach beyond words to express what we cannot say. We turn to another language—the language of symbol—to express the inexpressible. Giving a hug or a kiss, hearing a special song, seeing a team insignia, or noticing the flag flying at half-mast calls up a larger world of meaning that surpasses the everyday object itself.

From Gertrud Mueller Nelson, a liturgist, artist and mother, comes an image for what we are doing. She describes small children playing by the sea. Awed by the crashing power of the tremendous waves, they cling to their parents' legs. Then they do something that we may ourselves have done, that children have always done. They turn their backs "on what was too awesome" and dig a hole. Slowly they allow some of the great sea to fill the hole. It becomes their "mini-sea...a body of water that they could easily encompass and control." Sometimes the waves knock down the walls; "their manageable sea always lets in something of the unmanageable." But in the game, they "catch something of the transcendent."[2]

Nelson goes on to explain how the hole in the sea relates to a sacrament such as baptism. "In the same way we cannot head straight into the awe of the Almighty. Like the child before the ocean, we turn our backs on what is too much and slowly create the form that will contain something of the uncontainable. In faith, we make such ritual and are grateful for the discipline that form lends....In search of faith, indeed, in hope we make ritual. The power of the Almighty needs, sometimes, to be guarded against but it also needs to be beckoned, called forth and wooed."[3]

Over time, the intense love and longing that people felt for their children became encoded in a ritual like that of the children digging a hole by the sea. "Because symbols have this power to touch the entire range of our consciousness—rational thought, imagination, emotions, dreams—they are privileged means of expressing our most personal and important and disturbing experiences."[4] The feelings are as vast and powerful as giant waves. The ritual gives a form to help express and contain them. But just as the waves can always break into the hole, so the ritual is open to the transcendent, the great God who is at once beyond us and present to the tiniest detail of our lives.

What Makes a Catholic Uniquely Catholic?

Many would say it's our way of looking at the world sacramentally. We see God in our world, not only because God created it but also because God sustains it and acts in it now. The ability to see God as present and the world as good (flawed but still good) is an attitude absorbed early in life that becomes almost impossible to change.[5] The stance has been called "the Catholic imagination," and it models the attitude of Jesus. When he looked around—at sheep or vines or dough or lamps or mustard seeds—he saw more than the ordinary object. He saw how it revealed God, and he grounded his teaching in these things. So we too look for the "more," and are confident that this dimension beyond the object or event reveals God's presence in it.

If we develop the habit of seeking God's presence everywhere, then we can see how the most natural events are permeated with the divine. The sacraments lift up our already-graced experience. The simplest peanut-butter-and-jelly sandwich shared between parent and child has eucharistic overtones, and rain reminds us of baptism. We see in the efforts of good people to negotiate compromise the sacramental sign of reconciliation, and in a healthy marriage God's love for the church. If some places and events are especially sacramental, the reason is that everything is potentially sacramental.[6] To turn that around, if this piece of bread can become holy, should not all bread be reverenced?

In short, Catholics believe that there's always more to experience than meets the eye. What may appear to be a piece of bread is more—the outpouring of God's constant and abundant nurture. What seems like only a cup of wine is more—a steady and inspiriting stream from the God who made us and knows what we need. We are filled with wonder and awe at the universe because it bears the fingerprints of the God who created it. A later chapter describes the importance of nature as a way to find God.

So the sacraments celebrate what's already there. You have probably already had moments when you felt "touched by God"; perhaps when you met your spouse, learned you were going to have your child or saw your baby for the first time. All those joys are gathered up as God's people celebrate your delight in your child. They support your desires for that child to have the best of everything, including a centered, steady, spiritual core that can survive the roller coaster events that life will bring. You also want an identity that is larger than simply being the child of these parents at this time, but includes being part of a family that reaches around the globe and extends backward and forward for centuries in time. Just as you may have dreams about what this child will achieve in academics or sports, so also you may envision what he or she will do to model Christ, serve humanity and make the world a better place. All these surface in baptism. The question "What do you ask for your child?" could provoke not only a one-word answer, but unleash a whole tide of hopes, dreams and yearnings.

MARIANNE **Juan** Natasha
Michael Andrew Jennifer
Katherine Eugenis Polly
Gregory Kyle
Thomas Latisha
Oliver Drew Douglas SUE
Antonio Channel Jonathan
Gretchen
Bradley Perry
Alison Elizabeth

The question of your child's name is asked in baptism to mark a great adventure, to signal a personal relationship with God.

The Initial Questions of the Rite

What Name Do You Give This Child?

When we meet people at a party or at work, we often ask their names first. The name makes the person unique. It also gives us a certain hold on a person. Notice how quickly we respond if someone calls us by name; how skeptical we are of a phone solicitor who mispronounces our name or doesn't know it; how slow we are to answer if someone calls merely, "Madame?" or "Sir?"

If we know a person's name, we can command his or her attention. Hoping to improve his credibility with the Hebrew people, Moses asked God, "If they ask me, 'What is his name?' what shall I say to tell them?" (Exodus 3: 13). Knowing God's name places us in a more personal, intimate relationship than we might have with a distant, abstract deity.

But knowing a person's name is only the beginning of the conversation.

> Because after the exchange of names, the really difficult and fun part of life begins. It would be a little odd if, after the wedding, after the cake had been cut and the dances danced, the bride and groom fell into their chairs, looked at each other, and said, "Well, that was fun, wasn't it? I enjoyed that! Can I call you later?" "Call me?" the other would reply, "I'm going to move in with you!"
>
> And likewise, it would be odd if after the Easter Vigil [or Baptism], after the candle wax had been scraped off the floor and the incense smoke had cleared, Christians fell into their pews with the intention of calling God later. "Call me? If you'll have me, I'm moving in!" In Baptism we have given our name to God, and thereafter grace will pester us for the rest of our life until the church floor is littered with our bandages and sins and prejudices and miseries and jealousies and grudges. We will slough off our tomb apparel for the garment of immortality.[7]

The question of your child's name is asked in baptism to mark a great adventure, to signal a personal relationship with God. The people of God assembled here want to welcome this child as an individual. The leader asks much like the shepherd who knows each sheep by name (John 10:3). You've probably considered names for nine months, and finally fitted one, awkwardly or easily, onto this small

person. Perhaps the name honors a friend or relative, or joins a long list of family names.

Why did you choose your child's name? What does it mean to you?

Think for a moment how many times you will hear that name in the course of your child's life. You will call it in exasperation ("Dinner is getting cold!") or tenderness, ("Are you feeling better today?") and you will hear others call it on the playground, at doctor's offices and sporting events, at graduations and awards ceremonies, and later if your child makes a marriage vow. Your child will sign the name on library cards and school papers, on legal contracts and checks, on a voter's registration and a driver's license. In all the uses of the future, it will carry a special resonance for you. You chose it. You were the first to say it aloud.

Even before you named your child, God had a dream for that unique and irreplaceable person. From all eternity God imagined this individual, with these particular talents, genes, physical qualities and inner worlds. With the creator's delight, God said of your child, "I have called you by name, you are mine" (Isaiah 43:1). God declares at your child's baptism the same thing God did at the baptism of Jesus: "You are my child, the Beloved; with you I am well pleased" (Mark 1:11). Later in the baptismal rite, the presider will speak in the name of the Christian community, saying: "And in its name I claim you for Christ our Savior..." As in any relationship, name calls to name.[8]

Jesus receives his name not from his earthly parents but from God, his heavenly Father. God names and claims his Son. Jesus' name, from the Hebrew "Yahweh saves," reveals God's dream for his mission on earth. "Emmanuel" reminds us of his destiny to remain with us always.

> "She [Mary] will bear a son, and you are to name him Jesus, for he will save his people from their sins." All this took place to fulfill what had been spoken by the Lord through the prophet: "Look, the virgin shall conceive and bear a son, and they shall name him Emmanuel," which means, "God is with us" (Matthew 1:21-23).

What special divine blessing or destiny would you like your child's name to bring him or her?

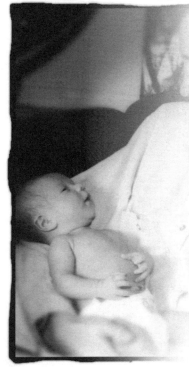

Like most symbols, naming has a history. In the earliest days of the Church, baptism was primarily for adults. They underwent a long period of preparation because the decision to become Christian could be a dangerous one, meaning they put their lives at risk. The first phase could last up to three years, and the second lasted forty days, the period of Lent. Entry into phase two began when they signed their names in a rite of enrollment. Thus, giving their names marked a transition to the final stage before baptism.

Unlike the choosing for sports teams or clubs, which can be cruel and exclusionary, God's choice never lifts anyone up by putting another down. To God, each individual name is special and precious. As Isaiah the prophet wrote: "The LORD called me before I was born, while I was in my mother's womb he named me" (Isaiah 49:1). The *Catechism of the Catholic Church* reminds us that "God calls each one by name. Everyone's name is sacred. The name is an icon of the person. It demands respect as a sign of the dignity of the one who bears it" (#2158).

Scripture contains many instances of persons who received new names to signal their new status in relationship with God. Read, for example:

Genesis 17:3-8, 15-16	Abram and Sari to Abraham and Sarah
Genesis 35: 9-15	Jacob to Israel
Matthew 16:13-19	Simon (Cephas) to Peter
Acts 9	Saul the persecutor to Paul the apostle

What Do You Ask of the Church for Your Child?

Most parents can quickly name what they want for their child in terms of personal relationships, athletic achievement, academic success, social life, financial security. Yet when we are asked to name what we want in that most intimate area of spirituality, we falter. If it helps, imagine your child at 75 or 80, surrounded by great-grandchildren. "I'm so grateful my parents gave me the faith," the old geezer says. "It has meant so much over my lifetime." What has it meant? Why do you want it for him or her? Why do you seek baptism or initiation into a faith community now?

Before going any further, write here what you want for your child in terms of faith development. If possible, share your responses with others in your baptismal preparation group.

While the following responses are hypothetical, they may represent a cross-section of different answers. None of them are definitive; all of them are right.

- "Grounding," one parent answers, "a sense of security."
- "Community," another says, "a network of people with similar values, a support system when things get tough."
- "A personal relationship or friendship with Christ," a third contributes.

As the conversation picks up energy, others chime in:

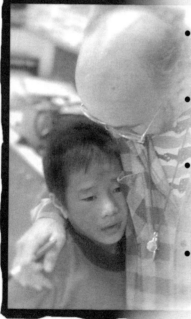

- "I grew up thinking God was out to get me. I was always terrified of being punished by God; most of my religion depends on guilt. I want something better for my daughter—maybe a kinder, more loving God."
- "I like a church that stands up for the voiceless and marginalized. I want my child to be part of a group that takes seriously its commitment to the poor."
- "My own family was kind of crazy—I want my child to be part of a larger family and relate to other people if I goof up."
- "I remember my grandma in her garden, always so serene and happy. Her life wasn't easy; I think her peace came from her religion. I want my kids to have whatever she had."
- "The neighborhood where I grew up was ugly and dangerous. But in church I could always find something beautiful: music, flowers, candles, stained glass, shiny gold or brass. Just being around it made me feel better for a little while. I want the same thing for my child: beauty."

In the rite of baptism, you will be asked this question. Most people respond with a one-word, ritual answer, such as "baptism" or "faith." But as we have seen, the one word is only a code for far more. Make sure you know what underlies your answer, so that it isn't rote or thoughtless. It is a question you may come back to over the years as your child's needs change. How will you answer at age 6? 16? 26? How might your child answer when he or she is old enough? The space below is left blank so you can record any thoughts you have about this question in later years. Come back to it on the anniversary of your child's baptism and compare: What in your answer has changed? What stays the same?

Remember too that your home is where your child will learn the earliest language of faith, and how to live as a follower of Jesus. Your home is a unique and intimate setting where your child will grow and develop in many important ways, long before he or she crosses the threshold of a religious education classroom or a school. Following Christ is not something that is taught all at once. It is modeled daily by your faith commitment

to living the gospel, as is signified in the baptismal ritual by your renunciation of evil and profession of faith.

The gospels reveal that our world is alienated from God through sin, dominated by the power of Satan, and engaged in a deadly struggle in which only the power of God through Christ can triumph. The lack of trust and disobedience that identifies all sin, whether personal or Original (that is, stemming from the sin of Adam and Eve; subjecting us to ignorance, suffering and death; and inclining us to sin), breaks down the harmony that God desired in creation.

In the *Rite of Baptism* you will be called on to renounce Satan and struggle against the tide of sin pulling us toward evil behavior. By renouncing Satan and professing your faith in Christ, you commit yourselves to creating and maintaining the right relationships with God and others. If you want to wisely protect vulnerable children in a world permeated by evil, you need to unmask its deceitful presence and name it.

What particular evils in your own life will come to mind as you do so?

The Symbols of Baptism

Remember the fairy tales where each visitor to the new child brings a gift? So too in the rite of baptism the

Church showers a lavish outpouring of gifts: incorporation into the life of the Trinity, welcome into the household of believers, Christ's victory over evil, eternal life, the deep joy and abiding peace of knowing we are always—whatever happens—in God's arms. Jesus himself promises that he will abide in us as we do in him (John 15:4). Through God's initiative (not our own) we are made into the very likeness of Christ (Vatican Council II, *Constitution on the Church, #7*).

But none of this happens in a few minutes. We are constantly learning how to "put on Christ," how to be conformed to his likeness. So too, the language for this event is symbolic—more than words could ever say. The poetry of faith is its symbols and stories, the reason for people's loyalty. Sociological surveys reveal that most Catholics remain Catholic not because of abstract doctrine but because of images established in childhood.

> Catholics stay in their Church because they like being Catholic, because of loyalty to the imagery of the Catholic imagination, because of pictures of a loving God present in creation, because of the spiritual vision of Catholics that they absorb in their childhood along with and often despite all the rules and regulations that were drummed into their heads.[9]

If the evocativeness of symbol and the cadence of story keep Catholics Catholic, then that seems like a good place in which to ground our understanding of baptism. Let us turn now to symbol and story.

> **"We ask you, Father, with your Son to send the Holy Spirit upon the waters of this font. May all who are buried with Christ in the death of baptism rise also with him to newness of life..."**
>
> —*Rite of Baptism, #91*

Water

Personal Reflection

Recall a time when you experienced the beauty or power of water. What happened? How did you feel at that time? Why do you suppose the experience has stayed in your memory?

Did the experience you recounted above contain both negative and positive elements? (For instance, water can cleanse and refresh, but also drown and destroy.) So, all the symbols can embrace polarities. For instance, fire can light and warm, but also burn and devastate. Such elemental forces are too vast to be pinned down to one narrow meaning, too huge to be confined by language.

The scriptures about water reflect the same combination of fear and delight. The blessing over the waters before your child's baptism will highlight the great water experiences of God's people. Biblical stories describe a passage through the terror of flooding to safety and liberation. For instance, the ark carried Noah and his family to a fresh beginning for the human race. The ark has since become a symbol for safety in chaos and a new start.

So too the Israelites passed through the Red Sea, leaving behind the slavery of Egypt. They responded to God's call to form a new community in which each person is committed to a new way of life.[10]

At his baptism, Jesus also makes a symbolic passage from death to life as his people had done before him. When John baptizes him in the river Jordan, he is immersed in waters that symbolize the primeval chaos, the floods that threatened Noah, the bondage of Egypt. He emerges to hear the voice of God calling him the beloved child, in whom God is well pleased. The stage is set for him to lead his people into a new covenant, in which God fulfills the divine promise to send a Messiah.[11]

The early Christians believed that those who did not live through the historical events could "recapitulate" them in a symbolic way to celebrate a birth from despair to hope,

slavery to freedom, failure to new possibility.[12] For them as for us, baptism represents a new beginning, full of freshness, freedom and creative potential—no matter how old we are!

Scripture

In the Bible, water is the ultimate symbol of life and death. In the parched and rocky Holy Land, water means life. Religious people look to God to supply what they need for living. On the journey from Egypt to the promised land, God provided food (Exodus 16, the quail and manna), water (Exodus 17:1-7) and protection from enemies (Exodus 17:8-14) so the Israelites could survive in the wilderness.

But water can also mean death when the dry ground cannot absorb the rain and floods career down valleys to destroy homes and villages. Since water is constantly changing, it also symbolizes the chaos out of which we are always trying to create our civilization (see Genesis 1). No wonder the ancients thought that God would destroy the world with a flood and return things to the original waters of chaos. When they pictured their situation, they symbolized their enemies as water and God's rescue as being saved from drowning.

You reached from on high and you grasped me;
you drew me out of deep waters.
You delivered me from my strong enemy,
and from those who hated me;
for they were too mighty for me...

You brought me forth into a broad place;
you delivered me because you love me.
(Psalm 18:16-18)

How has God entered to rescue you when you felt like you were drowning?

In anticipation of your child's baptism, read some or all of these biblical stories involving water. Also read them to your child as he or she grows old enough to enjoy them.

Genesis 6:5–9:17	Noah and God's great flood
Exodus 1–2; 13-15	Moses and the exodus through the waters of the sea. The water brings life for Israel and death for Egyptians.
2 Kings 5:1-14	Naaman a foreigner is cured of leprosy by washing in the Jordan River.
Mark 4:35-41	Jesus calms the storm at sea.
John 4:1-41	Jesus leads a Samaritan woman from talking about water to having faith in him.

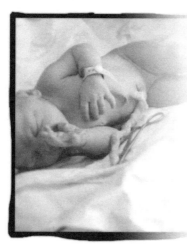

Ongoing Use of the Symbol

During the baptismal rite, the pouring of water or immersion in it is symbolic. In doing so we "immerse these little ones in the faith, in the grace, in the life of the One who loved them before time began, who loves them still, who will love them forever."[13] We immerse them into a pool of human kindness, represented by the people who gather around these waters.

Remember, in the space below or in conversation, your child's birth. Focus on the sense of new beginnings you had—both for your child and for yourself as a couple or family. What were your hopes and dreams as you saw your child for the first time?

Baptism is another birth; the water is like the amniotic fluid. The person is "born of God" into a much richer, larger life than we could imagine, that of God's daughter or son. Just as you recorded your dreams for your child in the space above, so God also has a vision for this child that surpasses anything we could ever name. God has a mission in mind, for which God has especially equipped your child with gifts and talents. Just as God chose for your child to be born into a specific human family with you as parents, so God also provides a larger family, one that stretches from the mountains of Japan to the shores of the Mediterranean, from the apartments of Manhattan to the barrios of Montevideo. The people who gather around the baptismal pool for your baby's baptism represent only a fraction of this larger mystical body, which stretches beyond our immediate time and space.

As your child grows, you can do some simple things together to relish water:

- Next time it rains, play outside in it. Splash in puddles, catch raindrops in your hands or on your lips, smell the freshness, watch the currents form in the gutters of the street. Sail boats, build dams, enjoy your child's delight.
- In a large bowl, add a cup of warm water to a packet of yeast. Watch the bubbles; enjoy the activity that water brings to what once was a lifeless powder.
- Make boats of Ivory soap. For a sail, punch three holes in a triangle of paper and thread a pipe cleaner through. Stick one end of pipe cleaner in the soap and float it in the tub.

- Water one plant and neglect another. Ask your child what happens when plants (or people) go too long without water.
- Repeat the old grade school science experiment: place several thicknesses of paper towel in a dish. Water it. Add a bean seed. Keep in a sunny window. Ask your child to keep the paper damp and to observe what happens.
- Play with the usual bath-time ritual. In the tub, place a sponge, soap, rubber duckie, shampoo, wash cloth, etc.—but no water! Ask your child, "What's wrong? Can you fix it?"
- During a child's bath play the "float and sink" game. Use items that float (like a cork, plastic ball, sponge) and items that sink (like a penny, spoon, clothes pin). Have the child experiment to find out which floats, which sinks.

- Mix water with Kool-Aid. Watch how the color spreads.
- Provide two large tubs of water, one clear and one soapy. Provide funnels, pitchers, measuring cups, spoons, etc. Let your child take the lead in playing with the water— or in cleaning all the toys. This is less messy outdoors in summer, but could conceivably be done on a linoleum floor in winter, with sponges and towels available for spills.
- Play outdoors with a bubble pipe or squirt bottles. Some of them are pretty elaborate now, but the old standbys are just as much fun.
- Fill various sized glasses or jars with different amounts of water. Enjoy the different pitches and sounds produced

when you "play" them by tapping on the glass or blowing air into them.

- Provide children with a bucket of water and a large paintbrush. Have them "paint" the outdoor walls of the house or the floor of the patio or deck. The surface color will change temporarily when it's wet.

- Walk around a lake or pond; notice the colors or reflections in the water. Sit or stand beside a stream or waterfall; listen to the music of the water.

- With your child, discover some of the other forms that water can take: snow, ice, icicles, water vapor, fog, dry ice. When your child gets to science class and hears that water can be gas, liquid or solid, he or she will nod knowingly.

Any of these activities would make a good preliminary to Praying with Water, p. 78.

Recall the symbol of water, especially during difficult times when money is tight, the temperature is too hot or too cold, nerves are frazzled, the appliances break down or the kids are fighting. Remember that God always pours grace as abundant as a waterfall on you and your child. Close your eyes, take a few deep breaths; imagine a beautiful waterfall. Savor the image; know that God's mercy is always close and always plentiful.

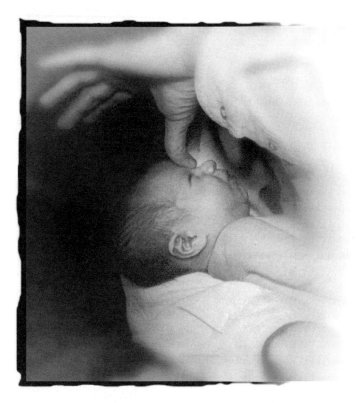

"I now trace the cross on your forehead, and invite your parents (and godparents) to do the same."

—*Rite of Baptism, #79*

Signing with the Cross

Personal Reflection

When has someone communicated an important message to you nonverbally? Describe that experience. Regardless of whether it was positive or negative, what did the gesture or touch communicate that words could not?

Who first taught you the sign of the cross? What memories cluster around this sign?

We may make the sign of the cross thoughtlessly if we don't think about all that it means. Signing with the cross gives a new identity—as a Christian who grounds faith firmly in Jesus' life and ministry. Because we bear his saving cross and share in his resurrection, our lives take on transcendent meaning and divine purpose.

Marked by that cross, we live like Jesus and adhere to the values of God's reign. The gifts freely poured on us in baptism give us the strength to stay faithful in suffering. We are called to mission, and know its high cost, the price Christ paid and the demands placed upon us.

In the Christian tradition, the cross symbolizes both death and victory, so for parents and godparents to thus mark their children can be "a marvelously shocking gesture." It says, "you are not only mine. You belong to Christ." Furthermore, we know that "only by way of the cross does this child's destiny include the glory of resurrection.

Parents represent the most fiercely instinctive urge of our species to protect the newborn." How can they then trace on the helpless child a symbol of capital punishment?[14]

We do so as part of a long tradition, remembering that even Mary and Joseph encountered threats to their new-born child. The words of Simeon must have shocked them when they brought their child to the temple, innocently following Jewish custom. Suddenly, his words cut into Mary's security: "a sword will pierce your own soul, too" (Luke 2:34). They fled to Egypt when a dream warned Joseph that King Herod would kill him (Matthew 2:13). And they worried intensely when they were separated from him in the temple, and feared him lost (Luke 2:43-45). If God's own Son was not immune to danger and threat, how could our children be any less vulnerable?

Scripture

There was nothing glorious about the cross in the ancient Roman world. Crucifixion involved a long and painful agony in which one's muscles became so rigid that breathing was impossible. The practice was forbidden to be used on Roman citizens, but its brutality sent a clear message to foreigners about Roman domination. Jesus' death sentence as king of the Jews is a warning of what rebellion against Roman authority will bring. Note that the gospels report no graphic details of Jesus' crucifixion. The horror of the cross would have been familiar to everyone.

After Jesus' death and resurrection, Christians turned this feared instrument of torture into a message of God's triumph over sin and death through Jesus. The domination of human empires is broken by the kingdom of God. The good news of Jesus' resurrection is that death ends only our earthly life, but not our relationship with God. Baptism plunges us into this mystery of death and life, apparent weakness and hidden triumph.

Jesus uses the image of carrying one's cross to describe the challenge of being his disciple. Imitation of Jesus demands following him through suffering and death into new life.

> *Then Jesus said to them all, "If any want to become my followers, let them deny themselves and take up their cross daily and follow me. For those who want to save their life will lose it, and those who lose their life for my sake will save it. What does it profit them if they gain the whole world, but lose or forfeit themselves?" (Luke 9:23-25)*

How do you make your most nagging daily crosses more bearable?

For other passages about the meaning of the cross, read:

1 Corinthians 1:18-25	The cross is a sign of God's wisdom and power.
Galatians 6:14	Paul boasts in Christ's cross.
John 20:24-29	Thomas is led to faith by touching Christ's nail wounds.
Colossians 2:12-15	Baptism lets us share in God's triumph through Jesus' cross.
Philippians 2:5-11	This is a poetic description of Christ's life and work with the cross at its center.

Ongoing Use of the Symbol

Make it a habit to trace a cross on your child's forehead regularly: perhaps at naptime, bedtime, mealtime, or as you bless an older child before going to day care, preschool or the playground. Teach your child to make the sign on him or herself, too. As they bless themselves with water entering a church, they are echoing two of the baptismal symbols.

When we bless our children with the sign of the cross, it's like handing on a family heirloom. As you do this, ask God for the grace to live fully in the present, appreciating what it means to be 8 or 18 months old, 40 days or 40 years old, so that if anything ever happens to this child or ourselves, we will have sadness, but we will not have regret. Ask also for the grace to see in our own suffering the outlines of Christ's cross. The pain won't necessarily end, but it will not be meaningless suffering because it is united to Jesus' saving action.

> **"As Christ was anointed priest, prophet and king, so may you live always as a member of his body, sharing everlasting life."**
> —*Rite of Baptism, #151*

Anointing with Oil

Personal Reflection

In the course of an ordinary day, how do you use oil?

What are the different purposes of oil?

We use oil for lubrication, protection, sun screen and fragrance. Babies smell especially good after a bath when their skins are sprinkled with baby powder, rubbed with lotions and oils. In the dry, hot, middle eastern climate, oil was vital for softening the skin and healing. It represented delight and refreshment to people.

In the contemporary setting of a children's book, a little girl remembers a person through the evocative action of applying lotion or oil:

> Before she died, I know my mother must have loved to comb my shiny hair and rub that Johnson's baby lotion up and down my arms and wrap me up and hold and hold me all night long. She must have known she wasn't going to live and she must have held me longer than any other mother might, so I'd have enough love in me to know what love was when I saw it or felt it again.[15]

In the Christian tradition, the Christ, the anointed one, came in beauty and fragrance. He was anointed priest, prophet and king as was his ancestor David. We continue that tradition with a post-baptismal anointing. One destined for God should be perfumed. "Animals know their young by smell. So too with us: Mother Church knows her newborns because they smell like Christ, like chrism, like glory."[16] The anointing of a child at baptism should be lavish, so everyone recognizes his or her royal lineage.

Scripture

The olive tree is the most common tree in Israel. It even survived the flood because Noah's dove comes back with a leaf from it! (Genesis 8:11). Olive oil was one of the staples of life. Its multiple uses for cooking, healing wounds, bathing, mixing with perfumes and especially for sacred anointing made it a rich symbol of human life.

Jesus is called the Messiah, a Hebrew word meaning "anointed." In Greek this is "christos," from which we get the word Christ. But Jesus' anointing in the gospels turned everything upside down (Matthew 26:6-13, Mark 14:3-9, Luke 7:36-50, John 12:1-8). Instead of being anointed by religious authorities in the temple to be a glorious king, he was anointed by a woman at a common meal as a sign of his suffering and death.

The Israelites mixed a special oil for anointing the temple and its sacred persons and objects. Anointing priests and kings with this sacred oil was a sign of their connection to God. They were chosen by God for their sacred roles, and God empowered them in their sacred duties.

Prophets were not anointed with oil but with the presence of God's Holy Spirit. This made them holy and signified their empowerment to speak God's word and do God's work. At a synagogue service, Jesus chose this passage from Isaiah, which sounds like a job description of a prophet, to usher in his own prophetic ministry (see Luke 4:16-30).

The spirit of the Lord GOD is upon me, because the LORD has anointed me; he has sent me to bring good news to the oppressed, to bind up the brokenhearted, to proclaim liberty to the captives, and release to the prisoners; to proclaim the year of the LORD's favor, and the day of vengeance of our God; to comfort all who mourn; to provide for those who mourn in Zion—to give them a garland instead of ashes, the oil of gladness instead of mourning, the mantle of praise instead of a faint spirit (Isaiah 61:1-3).

How does our anointing as Christians invite us to carry on Jesus' ministry of proclaiming good news and releasing people from what enslaves them?

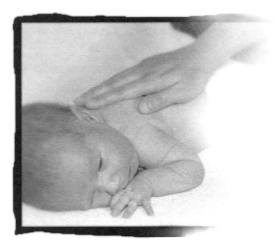

For other passages about oil, read:

Exodus. 30:22-32	Moses receives instructions for mixing the sacred oil for temple use (but don't try this recipe at home!).
1 Samuel 16:1, 6-7, 10-13	David is anointed as king.
Psalm 23	The Lord as shepherd anoints our head with oil.
Psalm 133	Oil is a symbol of family harmony.
Ephesians 1: 3-4, 13-14	God chooses us and marks us with the seal of the Holy Spirit.

Ongoing Use of the Symbol

Continue to anoint your child at home, using baby oil scented with a few drops of perfume. Make the sign of the cross on forehead or hands, so everyone (including your child) will know how important he or she is and discover what special talents have been given for the spread of God's reign. When family members are sick or sad, anoint them lavishly as a symbol of health and strength.

"You have become a new creation, and have clothed yourself in Christ. See in this white garment the outward sign of your Christian dignity. With your family and friends to help you by word and example, bring that dignity unstained into the everlasting life of heaven."

—Rite of Baptism, #99

New Garment

Personal Reflection

Remember getting a special, new piece of clothing. What made it unique? Where did you wear it? Why do you remember it?

As your child grows older, watch for the significance of clothes: the worn pj's he will not sleep without, the shirt with her favorite cartoon character, the souvenir of a trip, the new training pants or first pair of jeans like mom's or an older brother's, a winter coat saved for the first snowfall. One little girl made a ritual of cutting off the price tag, a gesture which meant that even the expensive dress couldn't be returned to the store. In the sacramental way of seeing things, it is not only the baptismal garment, but every garment that takes on significance.

Our identity is affected by what we wear—note how responsible the Marine captain looks in dress blues, how relaxed off duty in jeans and sweatshirt. When a doctor or nurse slips on a white jacket or green scrubs, it says something about the work they do—as do the firefighter's uniform, the judge's robes, or the clergy's vestments. So our identity as Christians is shaped at a deep level by the symbolic new garment.

After the water bath and anointing, we are not left wet and naked. Giving the new garment represents several things. One meaning echoes the wedding garment—just as a couple shares their life in marriage, so the newly baptized person shares in the life of Christ. Putting on the new garment signifies the new relationship (*Catechism of the Catholic Church*, #1243). In the early church, "'taking off the old self' (Colossians 3:9), or old clothes, was a comment on the pagan belief that evil spirits could cling to one's clothing like fleas."[19] The new garment also symbolizes Christian dignity. Finally, it stands for communion

with all Christians whose unseen "uniform" bonds them with Christ and each other. We clothe ourselves in Christ, and in all the kind deeds we do to his brothers and sisters.

Scripture

Like almost everything human, clothes convey meaning. Besides being useful for protection and warmth, they express who we are and what we want to be. When we change our clothes, we signal a change in ourselves. For jobs and sports, we put on uniforms and special clothing. For important occasions, like a wedding, we put on our best clothes.

Slogans and logos on clothes associate us with what they signify. So when we become Christians, we "put on Christ" (Romans 13:14) and associate ourselves with his mission and ministry. Like a good garment, Christ clothes us and makes us one.

> *But now that faith has come,...in Christ Jesus you are all children of God through faith. As many of you as were baptized into Christ have clothed yourselves with Christ. There is no longer Jew or Greek, there is no longer slave or free, there is no longer male and female; for all of you are one in Christ Jesus (Galatians 3:25-28).*

In what ways does Christ, like clothing, hide our differences and disunity?

For other passages about clothing ourselves for our God-given task, read:

Genesis 3:1-21	God clothes Adam and Eve after their sin.
Luke 15:11-32	The father clothes the returning prodigal son.
1 Samuel 17:1-51	David cannot fight Goliath dressed in King Saul's armor.
Isaiah 61:10	Salvation is pictured as God's clothing us.
Zechariah 3:1-4,	The high priests's new clothes signify removal of his guilt.
Ephesians 6:13-18	Christians put on the armor of God to struggle with evil.
Matthew 22:2-14	At the banquet of God's kingdom, we must wear our best clothing.

Ongoing Use of the Symbol

Some families have a special baptismal gown, on which they embroider the name and baptismal date of every baby baptized in it. If you have such a gown, continue the tradition. If not, consider starting one or adapting the idea. Make sure you take out this gown on the anniversary of the baptism for your child to admire (see Praying with the Baptismal Garment, p. 81).

Any time your child is especially excited about getting new clothes is a "teaching moment." In the context of that excitement, you might reminisce about the tiny garment which symbolized how he or she "put on Christ." If your child confronts a difficult situation—for instance, a bully in day care or preschool—remind the child how he or she is clothed in an invisible garment of strength and kindness. Say something like this: "Close your eyes and imagine that you are wearing a beautiful white garment. It shines like the sun on a stream. The person who wears it is big and strong and kind. So are you."

> "Receive the light of Christ. Parents and godparents, this light is entrusted to you to be kept burning brightly. This child of yours has been enlightened by Christ. He/she is to walk always as a child of the light. May he/she keep the flame of faith alive in his/her heart. When the Lord comes, may he/she go out to meet him with all the saints in the heavenly kingdom."
>
> —*Rite of Baptism, #100*

Handing on of the Candle

Personal Reflection

There are many ways that a light can penetrate a darkness. Recall an experience when you really appreciated light in the dark, such as a bonfire, candlelight dinner, vigil, concert, or a flashlight during a power outage. Describe it here.

Recall a time when you had an insight that helped you understand causes, connections or relationships, perhaps at work or in a conversation. We refer to such a moment as "then the light bulb went on," or "suddenly I saw the light!" Briefly describe that time here.

During the rite of baptism, a smaller candle is lit from the Easter candle to signify that Christ enlightens our minds and hearts as did the light in the experiences described above. The baptismal candle symbolizes not only that Jesus is the light of the world, but also, as Matthew 5:14 proclaims, that we are the light of the world. Just as Christ enlightens the minds and hearts of the baptized (*Catechism of the Catholic Church,* #1243), so we in turn bear the light of Christ to illuminate whatever darkness we confront.

Candlelight holds a natural fascination for young children. Knowing that they too are light empowers them to make a difference in a dark world. During dark times—of tension, grief, anger or uncertainty—draw on this symbol. Imagine a light so strong it dispels all darkness: this is the power of Christ.

Scripture

Light is associated with God's presence and often accompanied an appearance of God, for example, when God appeared to Moses in the burning bush (Exodus 3:1-15) and on Mt. Sinai (Exodus 19:16-19) or when Christ appeared to Saul on the way to Tarsus (Acts 9:1-20). Fire is an appropriate reminder that light is beneficial, but is also dangerous. It is often difficult to control and changes completely whatever it touches.

As Psalm 27:1 reminds us, when we walk in God's light, nothing can disturb us because everything is illuminated. "The LORD is my light and my salvation; whom shall I fear? The LORD is the stronghold of my life; of whom shall I be afraid?" Jesus, who is the human image and revelation of God, shares the divine light. Thus he becomes "the light of the world" (John 8:12) and brings God's light so that we will not walk in darkness.

In the beginning was the Word, and the Word was with God, and the Word was God. He was in the beginning with God. All things came into being through him, and without him not one thing came into being. What has come into being in him was life, and the life was the light of all people. The light shines in the darkness, and the darkness did not overcome it (John 1:1-5).

In what ways has Jesus broken into your darkness to bring you light?

For other passages about light, read:

Genesis 1:1-5	God creates light first.
Luke 9:28-36	Jesus is transfigured.
Matt. 5:15 -16	Let your light shine for others.
Luke 8:16-17	Nothing remains hidden from God's light.
John 12:35-36	Jesus invites us to walk in the light.
Ephesians 5:8-14	We are children of light.
1 John 1:5-7	God is light.
1 Peter. 2:9	God calls us into the light.

Ongoing Use of the Symbol

Every year on the anniversary of the baptism, light the child's baptismal candle, reminding the child of this calling to be light in the world. To preserve it for several years, let it burn only a few minutes. The sense that it is precious and scarce will reinforce for your child the idea that it is special. This is also a good time to sing "This Little Light of Mine." Use other candles at other prayer times, noting their quieting, centering effect. During Advent, light one candle each week to symbolize how time draws near the coming of Jesus, the light of the world, at Christmas.

"If possible, baptism should take place on Sunday, the day on which the Church celebrates the paschal mystery. It should be conferred in a communal celebration for all the recently born children, and in the presence of the faithful, or at least of relatives, friends, and neighbors, who are all to take an active part in the rite."

—*Rite of Baptism, #32*

The Assembled Community

Personal Reflection

List names of people who were important to you as you were growing up.

List names of people you hope will play similar roles for your child.

The community is a central symbol for any sacrament, but especially for baptism. We don't come to God alone; the baptismal waters are our birth into the family of God. This is not a random collection of people; the Greek word for "assembly" is *ekklesia,* "called together." God gathers those joined to Christ for a special purpose. They witness through their faith and promise their support to the baptized child. Through baptism, one enters the life of this community, shares in its faith and takes on the responsibility of bearing that faith to others. "Without faith, sacraments become magical gestures; without community, they are reduced to a privatistic and individualistic form of religious behavior that is contrary to our entire tradition."[20]

The assembly includes not only the people who are visible at this particular gathering but also a larger, unseen group. The community of saints extends beyond our immediate place and time, to include Christians throughout the world and those who have gone before us in death. As a parent, it is consoling to know that you are not alone. A universal community, both seen and unseen, collaborates on behalf of your child.

This community believes that it is not possible to live well in a complex world without the Christ who has triumphed over death. His death and resurrection make it possible for us to try to be like him, to overcome our limitations and to rise after our own deaths. This group of people who remember Jesus in the very fiber of their beings "live radically different lives, staking everything on the promise of the resurrection."[21]

While the promise may seem bold and the response risky, for centuries it has helped people in this community struggle to freedom from the burden of oppression, like their ancestors in faith who fled from Egypt through the Red Sea and are commemorated in the prayer blessing the baptismal waters. It gives them a clear direction and a secure stance when life's upheavals become especially rough.

Bringing your child to this community for baptism renews its own identity and purpose. That is why their procession from the door to the font to the altar is symbolic. It represents a people who are never static but always on the move—just as were their Hebrew ancestors in the desert or the disciples on the road to Emmaus. Their actions of gathering, processing, voicing beliefs and making promises are as vital to them as they are to your child.

Practical Preparations

Your group discussions, your reading and reflecting, your gratitude to God for your new child, all these combine in preparation for your baby's baptism. Here are a few practical details you may want to consider before the event.

1. Read over what you have written in response to the two questions that will be asked during the rite (see pp. 16, 19). These reflections will prepare you for the public response.

2. To enhance the celebration, Gaynell Cronin and Jack Rathschmidt make these suggestions.[22] Consider whether you'd like to implement any or all of them and discuss the possibilities with your parish staff.

   A. Parents carry their lighted wedding candle in procession and light the Easter candle from it.

   B. Both sets of grandparents bring water from their homes and pour into the baptismal font as a symbol of all they share with their grandchild.

   C. Have a cup inscribed with your child's name to pour the baptismal waters. When the child can drink from a cup, encourage him or her to use it daily.

3. Consider including in the Litany of Saints the saint for whom the child is named, the parents' and godparents' favorite saints, and any others you wish the child to imitate.

4. If possible, ask that representatives like the grandparents or godparents prepare and read the scriptures of the day and participate in the presentation of gifts.

5. If this is too time-consuming during the baptism, consider doing it during an informal session before or after the baptism. Ask the guests to explain briefly what it means to each of them to be a disciple of Christ, and how their special form of discipleship can be a gift to the child.

Any liturgical celebration is only a part of a larger reality, a process that continues gradually over a long period of time. An actual baptism takes only a few minutes, but it may take a lifetime to understand and appreciate its meaning. So in the next section, we turn to the time after baptism and the long-range preparations for first eucharist.

During those years, use this guide as a memory book and a help toward nurturing your child's spirituality. You may wish to read it in small sections; don't feel overwhelmed or think that you must do everything it suggests at once.

Notes

1. Thomas Morris, *The RCIA: Transforming the Church* (New York: Paulist Press, 1997), 29.
2. Gertrud Mueller Nelson, *To Dance with God* (New York: Paulist Press, 1986), 25.
3. Ibid., 26.
4. Bernard Cooke, *Sacraments and Sacramentality* (Mystic, CT: Twenty-Third Publications, 1985), 45.
5. Andrew Greeley, *The Catholic Myth* (New York: Charles Scribner's Sons, 1990), 49.
6. Andrew Greeley and Mary Durkin, *How to Save the Catholic Church* (New York: Viking, 1984), 47.

7. David Fagerberg, "Call Me by Name," *U.S. Catholic*, September 1999, 45.
8. Catherine Dooley, "Mystagogy: Ministry to Parents," in Victoria Tufano, ed., *Catechesis and Mystagogy: Infant Baptism* (Chicago and Allen, TX: Liturgy Training Publications and Tabor Publishing, 1996), 103.
9. Greeley, *The Catholic Myth*, 63.
10. Monika Hellwig, *The Meaning of the Sacraments* (Dayton, OH: Pflaum, 1981), 7.
11. Ibid., 9.
12. Ibid., 9.
13. David Philippart, "A Homily for the Baptism of Children," in *Catechesis and Mystagogy*, 78.
14. Robert Duggan, "Infant Baptism and the Process of Christian Initiation," in *Beginning the Journey: From Infant Baptism to First Eucharist* (Washington, DC: U.S. Catholic Conference, 1994), 7.
15. Cynthia Rylant, *Missing May* (New York: Orchard Books, 1992), 4.
16. Philippart, *Catechesis and Mystagogy*, 72-73.
17. J. Robert Baker, Larry J. Nyberg, Victoria M. Tufano, eds., *A Baptism Sourcebook* (Chicago: Liturgy Training Publications, 1993), 132. St. Ambrose lived from 339-397 A.D.
18. Ibid., 189. St. Augustine lived from 354 to 430 A.D.
19. Bill Dodds, "Baptism Comes Full Circle," *Catholic Digest*, June 1999, 46.
20. Duggan, *Beginning the Journey*, 10.
21. Hellwig, *The Meaning of the Sacraments*, 10.
22. Jack Rathschmidt and Gaynell B. Cronin, *Rituals for Home and Parish* (New York: Paulist Press, 1996), 51-53.

Part 2

And Beyond: Nurturing Your Child's Spirituality

Giving the infant room to roll over and to watch stimulating mobiles or colorful shapes means that the toddler will eventually be able to propel, wash, feed and dress himself or herself... Wholeness is the first step to holiness.

Chapter 2

The Spirituality of Children

In the space below, attach your child's footprint or handprint that was made in the hospital. Or, make the imprint now by using a stamp pad, then immediately cleaning off the baby's hand or foot. Use the stamp pad to make other handprints or fingerprints of significant people in this child's life: parents, godparents, siblings or grandparents. Place these around your child's print.

As you look at the prints above, notice how each is unique, yet each is distinctly human. If you inserted a bear's pawprint here, the difference would be obvious! So too the spirituality of each person is unique. Yet, your baby's spirituality will be affected by you as surely as your genes influence his or her coloring, height, or facial features. This chapter will consider your child's spirituality, not in isolation, but in connection with your own.

A Parent's Spirituality

Few parents would refuse to feed a hungry child. Yet many parents are unsure how to nurture a child's spiritual hungers. Some may not even know what they are. One way to tap into these desires is by remembering your childhood. Did you have longings you could not voice, a desire for something you could not explain even to those who were closest? Perhaps you recall a snatch of music, the sound of a certain voice, a glimpse of the night sky, a fascination with a spider web or an affection for a certain blanket or stuffed animal. Maybe a particular smell or taste evoked an inexplicable yearning—not for any food or toy or experience that a parent could provide, but for something beyond all that, not sold at any store.

Some theologians call this "desire for I know not what" an echo of God's desire that creates us and sustains us in being. God brings us into existence and plants in our hearts a deep thirst for the All, the great mystery, the infinite love.[1] God is the source of what we most desire and the reason for our being.

Use the space below to record your own memories of childhood longings that are hard to explain, but might be called spiritual hungers.

How can we get in touch with a child's spirituality if we're out of touch with our own? Just as a mother protects the fetus during pregnancy by avoiding drugs or alcohol, so too the birth of a child calls for many changes in lifestyle. Besides giving up sleep and adjusting schedules, one vital change may be to find more quiet time for reflection. Life gets busier with children, which is all the more reason to slow down. Ask what can be eliminated from your schedule to give the child (and yourselves!) more time and peace. It isn't necessary to enroll your growing child in every imaginable activity. Quiet, empty time and reflection are essential for the spiritual health of both children and adults.

Use the space below for your own "spiritual profile." What are your strengths in this area? Describe the faith you have inherited from your family of origin. What elements of it would you like to pass on to your child?

The Parent's Role

As with every other facet of child development, the parent's role changes as the child grows. Initially, the child learns all he or she needs to know about God and humanity from the parent: that mom or dad can be trusted, that an expression of need will be answered, and that someone will respond to the most basic attempts to communicate. At a time when the child is immensely vulnerable, the parent's voice and touch reassure that she is not alone, that someone will care for him. The parent who tires of diaper changes or 2 a.m. feedings should know the importance of these seemingly mundane tasks. They are more than physical chores; they teach a child the most basic lesson of trust, without which future growth is difficult or impossible.

From birth to about age three, the parent's most natural actions, even those we take for granted, establish the foundation for faith development. By providing opportunities for the child's large and small motor activity, the parent sets the stage for later growth in independence and self-confidence. Giving the infant room to roll over and to watch stimulating mobiles or colorful shapes means that the toddler will eventually be able to propel, wash, feed and dress himself or herself. The parent who cheers for the first bites of solid food or first tiny steps will see the fruits of this encouragement in a toddler who has a strong self-image. Wholeness is the first step to holiness.

Other areas parents can influence are the development of language and the security of routine. Children learn language at a rate that is unsurpassed throughout the rest of their lives. Parents who talk with their children, read to them and help them name objects give them a head start on later schooling. Providing experiences now (such as those in Chapter 5 on Children and Nature) gives them the basis later for learning to read.

Simple routines in the home give children a sense of stability, a sense that the world is a secure place. Because repetition is so important, children will cling to it in a way that can drive their parents crazy. It is understandable—adults are much the same. We establish the teeth-brushing, face-washing, coffee-drinking routine of the morning so firmly that it requires little thought. We soon learn that for children, bedtime must proceed in the same way every night—deviate an inch and risk a night's sleep!

The importance of the parents' role in these first three years cannot be overestimated. If the groundwork for healthy human development is not laid during these "golden years," it is almost impossible to establish later. The sad stories of children neglected or abused during infancy give eloquent testimony to this truth, unfortunately from the negative side. From a positive angle, a happy toddler who has been well-loved and nurtured confirms the observation of St. Irenaeus that the glory of God is a human being fully alive.

From the age of three on, the toddler's curiosity blossoms. While it may unnerve the parent at times, it is an inborn gift. It leads the child to use all the senses to explore the world and grapple with its intriguing mysteries. Older children take pride in their responsibilities at home (tasks suited to their developmental level) and in their widening social circles (play groups, preschool, day care, etc.). This is also an ideal time to encourage the child's religious imagination.

Encouraging the Religious Imagination

Few parents would argue with the idea that young children have vivid imaginations. Watch their eyes widen at things adults ordinarily take for granted: lightning, dew, the spiral of a cinnamon roll, the rainbow that dark oil reflects in a puddle, bugs, feathers, pebbles and fur.

Sophisticated media are also aware of the child's imagination. They appeal to it through movies, television, advertising, because the appeal can be direct and visceral. It bypasses words and ideas to approach the child in a vulnerable and easily impressionable place. Listen to any preschooler hum the theme from the latest television show or advertising slogan. Watch as they model their favorite cartoon characters. Their T-shirts often display the face or logo of a favorite athlete or team. In later years, they fervently admire sports figures or movie stars and are firmly convinced that they too can become the stars of the playing field or screen.

This natural aptitude can be turned to the religious imagination. Parents interested in encouraging a child's spirituality can appeal to the imagination on the same grounds as the media—not necessarily with words and ideas, but with symbols and stories (see Chapter 1 on symbol and Chapter 4 on storytelling for more on these). For heroic models of being a Christian, children have a rich heritage in the saints.

The Community of Saints

These role models are known not for their prowess with a baseball, but for their kindness and compassion. In the Christian tradition, we hold up the saints as Christians to admire. Some are officially recognized as saints (canonized); others are held sacred in personal or family memory. Think for a moment about those you would name "saint"; perhaps a teacher who encouraged you, a grandmother who always had a welcoming lap and listening ear, a friend who challenged you to continue education or leave a deadening job. Sometimes people name their children after the people who have meant so much to them. Others tell their children the story of "the man who first gave me a job" or the "librarian who saved special books for me." They don't necessarily have the highest I.Q. or the largest incomes, but their warmth and basic goodness stay with us for years as examples of how we think Jesus would have acted.

Name here the people who have been most influential in your life. Which quality of theirs is most outstanding? What would you like your child to know about these saintly people?

Guiding Principles of Children's Spirituality

Research in the field of children's spirituality offers several principles helpful to parents for guiding this intimate, mysterious development in the life of their child. It is inspiring to think that our children are engaged in a process like that of the boy Jesus: "And Jesus increased in wisdom and in years, and in divine and human favor" (Luke 2:52).

1. The Child Has a Deep Longing for God

Any parent knows how a child can be greedy for love—often needing more love and attention than a human parent can provide! This points to the need for a God who is infinite love. This divine parent never gets tired or cranky like a human parent does; this is the parent the child deserves —"a God ready to forgive, gracious and merciful, slow to anger and abounding in steadfast love" (Nehemiah 9:17).

Sofia Cavalletti concluded from her studies of three and four-year-olds that the child's relationship with God manifests itself in "a joy that appears to touch the deepest part of the child." Even in children who had little or no religious upbringing, she found attractions to religious realities existing before any adult prompting.[2]

2. The Child Asks Eternal Questions

Children have a knack of asking questions that have concerned the finest human minds since time began. Who am I? Where did I come from? Where am I going? A child's silence or art work can contain deep thoughts that his or her language is not developed enough to express. At such times, the proper stance for the parent is humility before children's "exquisitely private" moments of "awe and wonder and alarm and apprehension."[3]

3. Wonder with Your Child

The most productive approach for a parent is probably that of wondering and speculating with a child. To hand

down information simply squelches the child's natural inquisitiveness. To respect the child's questions encourages the child to ask more. Children will ask questions about things that puzzle our deepest thinkers: Why did grandma have to die? What will happen to me if I am left alone? What if we have a war?

Most parents have been driven crazy by endless variations of questions like "Why is the sky blue?" But the alternative—a child who asks no questions—is far worse because it suggests a deadened imagination, without the natural birthrights of wonder and awe.

4. The Child Expresses Religious Truths Concretely

While any relationship with God is mysterious, children try to express the mystery in concrete ways. In short, their faith is grounded in the here-and-now, sense perceptible realities of their daily experience. The research of David Heller suggests children are less interested in formal liturgy than in belief expressed in everyday ways. They depict God as intimately involved in family life, a fact which creates an entry point for parents. Parents are the most logical people to seize those close-at-hand moments. An attentive parent can pick up on what's happening immediately. A child's remark that may seem illogical or thoughtless to a disinterested observer may reveal to a caring parent a whole inner world. For instance, the real question underlying "Where do dogs go when they die?" may be the haunting question of "What happens to me after death?"

The concrete thinking of children is also a natural link to understanding the sacraments. Abstract concepts, like grace, salvation, and forgiveness, are learned through flowing water, lavish oils, compassionate touch, nurturing bread and wine.

Images of God

When you were a child, how did you imagine God?

If you answered "an old man with a white beard," you are not alone. Many people grew up with this image of God. But as your child grows, you may want him or her to have a broader range of images to turn to as the need for a different image of God arises. Not that God is a chameleon, who changes according to our whim, but God has an infinite variety of faces and voices and reveals the one that we most need at the time.

While God is a mystery that we can never define (the root of the word *define* means to set limits!), we *can* say "God is like..." Here are some images of God presented in the Bible.

an eagle (Deuteronomy 32:11-12)

a shield (Psalm 3:3)

a hostess (Proverbs 9:5)

a rock and fortress (Psalm 18:2)

a mother bear (Hosea 13:8)

a tower and refuge (Psalm 61:3)

a father (Luke 11:2)

a mother hen (Matthew 23:37)

a shepherd (John 10:11)

a vine (John 15:5)

a comforting mother (Isaiah 66:13)

a gate (John 10:9)

light (John 8:12)

You and your child can look up one of these images, draw it, act it out or mime it. If you feel uncomfortable with this kind of movement, remember that "children are like dancers: only in their movement are children deeply themselves."[4]

For example, if God is like an eagle, how would the wings move? If God is like a mother bear, how does God cradle the young? If God is like a mountain, how does God stand? If God prepares a feast for us, what does God set on the table? If God is like a shepherd, how does God walk with the sheep? How does God look when sheltering young chickens like a mother hen? If God is like the vine and we are like the branches, how do we grow together?

In the following space, a child may draw a favorite image of God. Or a parent may draw the child doing one of the movements suggested above.

My Favorite Image of God

If your child resonates with a particular image of God, reinforce it. For instance, if your child likes the image from Psalm 3 that "The Lord is my shield," look for pictures of shields in books at the library or at an art museum. Draw an outline of a shield, make several copies of it and encourage your child to decorate each one in a different way. Or make one from cardboard. Your child may want to cut out shields and hang them around a bed, a room or a kitchen. Talk about what a shield represents—protection and security—and how God protects and shelters us from harm.

At some time your child may want to move on to another image. If he or she likes the image of God as a mother hen, again find pictures or point out hens and chickens at a farm or zoo. Talk about how the mother hen treats her chicks and connect this with how God cares for us in the same way.

Praying with the baptismal symbols will also open up many images for God: as being like light, water, oil, clothing and community. Ways to pray with these images are suggested in Chapter 3.

To summarize this chapter, here are five Do's and Don'ts for Parents:

Five Do's

1. Respect and nurture your child's privacy. We all need a little quiet time alone to think without intrusions. As your child outgrows naps, provide quiet times in which inner resources can develop. If you have more than one child, look for opportunities to take one-on-one time with each child.

2. Realize that your child has a larger repertoire of knowledge than can be expressed in verbal statements. Look beyond words to other vehicles of expression: movement, art, silence, questions. In short, "read between the lines" to discover the meaning your child is discovering.

3. Expect a correlation between your child's relationship with you as parent and your child's relationship with

God. If you are caring and forgiving, your child will see God the same way.

4. Adopt a stance of "speculating together" rather than one of having all the answers. Few adults do, so let's be honest. We can tell our children what we believe or stories about our own lives without becoming dogmatic or forcing them to believe what we do.

5. Remember that children have a profound capacity for imitation. (Consider the phenomenon of wearing the baseball cap backwards!) You can talk all you want about religion, but your actions will drown out the words. Just as most people choose a college major or a career because a person close to them influenced them in that direction, so too most people come to faith through the influence of another—often a parent.

Five Don'ts

1. Don't project your own spiritual state onto your child. Simply because you are joyous, perplexed, angry or numb doesn't mean your child is.

2. Don't expect adult religious abstractions from children. They may express some deep insight or profound thought through concrete, direct language or questions.

3. Don't underestimate your child. More may be occurring beneath the surface than appearances reveal. Likewise, don't assume your child is always happy. He or she may be grappling with deep and difficult questions while

lacking the concepts and words to describe what is going on.

4. Don't worry about a magical component in your child's thinking about faith or God. Under the age of eight, magical qualities are natural because the world seems under the control of larger, more powerful beings. Magic seeks to manage these powerful forces and bring them under our control. On the other hand, don't play into it with too many stories of Jesus' healing or walking on water. The concept of Jesus as magician will be less central as they mature, but Jesus as compassionate seeker for the lost will endure.

5. Don't relegate religion to Sunday only. Religion should be integrated with the rest of life or its effect will be minimal. Encourage spontaneous conversation with God—for instance at mealtime or when noticing something beautiful in nature. Few friendships could grow in an hour a week; so building a friendship with God flourishes when it's given plenty of time and reinforcement.

Use the space on the next page to record statements or questions your child has made about God, life/death or any other spiritual issues. Be sure to record the date to help you remember how old he or she was at the time.

My Child's Questions about God

Notes

1. William Barry, *What Do I Want in Prayer?* (New York: Paulist Press, 1994), 27-28.
2. Sofia Cavalletti, *The Religious Potential of the Child* (New York: Paulist, 1983), 32, 36.
3. Robert Coles, *The Spiritual Life of Children* (Boston: Houghton Mifflin, 1990), 36-37.
4. Mary Catherine Berglund, "Obeying the Mystery: Worship and the Very Young," in *Beginning the Journey* (Washington, DC: U.S. Catholic Conference, 1994), 44.

**The child's work is to grow,
and the means for this
growth is the senses.**

—*Jerome Berryman*

Chapter 3

Praying with Children

As we saw in the previous chapter, our children already have a deep spirituality. Our task as parents is awakening and nurturing it. One way to do so is to encourage that ongoing conversation with God called prayer. Hearing or reading that word, many people will immediately picture people kneeling in pews at church, silent or reciting formal words together. That may be one easily recognizable form of prayer, but surely there are many kinds of conversation between a God who loves us passionately and God's daughters and sons. If this is true for adults, it is also true for children.

Those who study children's spirituality say that children's prayer may not take the easily recognizable, "standard" form. For a child, play can be prayer—as can movement, rapt absorption in art, wonder at nature, imagination, music, listening to stories, or silence. Taking prayer seriously means getting comfortable with silence, even for a long period. Children growing up in a constantly noisy world of radio, television, telephone and traffic need quiet times and spaces throughout the day for reflection. By including a quiet time in the daily schedule, you help your child grow into the kind of centered, thoughtful, steady person most adults want to be around. We all stumble into mystery, but if you feel uncomfortable with quiet, let your child be your guide. He or she may be more at ease than you anticipate.

Praying with the Baptismal Symbols

"The child's work is to grow, and the means for this growth is the senses. If you want to meet the child's deepest need to grow, then you need to play with the child in a sensorial way."[1] Using sense-ible things that can be seen, heard, touched, smelled and tasted is also a good way to start prayer. Fortunately, the Catholic tradition is "earthy," which appeals to a child's attraction to the concrete. We have always used material things: bread, wine, oil, water, colors, fire, ashes, palms and incense in our worship. These always symbolize more than we can say in words.

So too with children. Concrete things help focus attention, but a child can also see beyond the signs to the deeper realities that they stand for. (Doesn't your child know what it means when you hold hands with someone? Or when you frown? So too, a child can easily learn to make a connection between a concrete object and the larger, intangible world it represents.) As your child matures and grows in appreciation for what baptism means, praying with its symbols may be helpful. "It would be difficult to avoid abstractionism if the signs did not render baptismal theology so visible and tangible."[2]

Water

To prepare for this prayer you will need a child's Bible or storybook, a bowl, and a pitcher full of water.

Tell or read one of the water stories from scripture, such as God creating the world and seas (Genesis 1: 6-11), Noah and the ark (Genesis 6:5–9:17), the parting of the Red Sea (Exodus 14:10-31), Moses striking the rock so people have water to drink (Exodus 17:1-7), Jesus' baptism (Mark 1:4-11), Jesus calming the storm at sea (Mark 4:35-41) or Jesus and the woman at the well (John 4). Invite your child to draw a picture of one or more stories in the space below, or to act it out as you reread it.

My Drawing of a Water Story

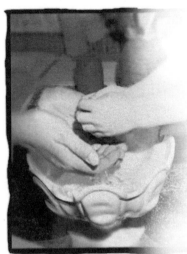

Fill a bowl (if possible, a special, beautiful bowl) with water. Dip your hands in it, pouring water yourself and inviting the child to pour water. Then bless each other with it, using each other's names: "I bless you in the name of the Father, the Son and the Holy Spirit. Amen."

Sit in silence for a few moments, appreciating the water. If your child wishes to talk about it, fine, but do not force conversation.

Sign of the Cross

At times you may wish to bless your child with oil, another baptismal symbol. If so, you will need a small container of oil, if possible, scented with perfume.

Make the sign of the cross on your child every night when he or she goes to bed, or at another regular time if bedtime is inconvenient. Your child will learn from the reverence of your touch that this is a special mark. Through this sign, he or she is claimed for Christ Jesus, set apart to do wonderful works for God and shielded from evil by God's protection.

New Garment

To prepare for this prayer, you will need a favorite blanket or shirt, selected by your child, and your child's baptismal garment.

Ask your child to choose a favorite blanket, sweatshirt or T-shirt. Wrap the child gently in it. Ask, "how do you feel when you are wrapped in your favorite blanket or clothing?" You might expect or elicit responses such as, "warm," "comfy," "safe" or "happy." Continue to cuddle your child in this garment as you look at the white baptismal garment.

Ask the child what it looks like, or say something like this:

> How small it is—look how much bigger you are have grown since you first wore it!

> How white and clean and beautiful it is! It shows the light that is in our hearts. It helps us remember that we are always wrapped in Jesus. He is as close to us as the clothing touching our skin. He is as warm and safe as your favorite blanket, sweatshirt or T-shirt.

Light/Candle

Prepare for this prayer by having a large candle , a small candle and matches. Cut a small circle of cardboard and make a hole in its center for the small candle to fit through. This will protect your child's hand from hot wax drips while holding the candle. On the anniversary of your child's baptism, make the prayer special by using the baptismal candle.

Tell about a time when you were afraid in the dark. Ask your child about a time when he or she was afraid in the dark.

Then reverently light the large candle. Say, "When Jesus came, he drove away the darkness. He took fear away. Now he brings light into our hearts. He asks us to be like him, the light. He tells us, 'you are the light of the world' (Matthew 5:14)."

Light your child's small candle from the large one. Your child can hold the small candle safely and carefully if you have placed the cardboard around it so that it is above your child's hand.

Sit in silence for a few moments appreciating the glow of the candles. If your child wishes to speak, fine, but do not force a conversation.

Introduce all the other baptismal symbols gradually, praying with each one individually. Then invite your child to draw his or her baptism in the space below, including the large and small candles, the water, oil, sign of the cross and new garment.

My Baptism

Prayer with Other Natural Objects

Isaac blessed his son Jacob with these words:

> "May God give you of the dew of heaven,
> and of the fatness of the earth, and plenty of grain
> and wine." (Genesis 27:28)

Like Issac's blessing, prayer with children can celebrate the good gifts of the Creator.

You and your child may want to have a special prayer corner or prayer table where you can keep important objects that prompt prayer. Your child might choose a pine cone from a Christmas tree, a stone, seed, shell, flower or feather found on a walk, a picture or postcard. These may change over time as the objects lose their novelty—or your child may want to keep them long after you have grown tired of them. Let your child replace them as the need arises.

Record here something your child has said about prayer with natural objects.

Draw here or place photographs of two or three of God's good gifts you've found.

Gifts I've Found

Daily Prayer

Remember that different people like different kinds of prayers. We all choose different friends, spouses, children's names and clothes, so why should we all pray the same way? The important thing is that God welcomes all the voices of God's children. If your child wakes you in the middle of the night, your first reaction may be annoyance. But underneath that, you are glad that your child is alive and well. So God is delighted to hear from us, no matter how awkward we feel or how strained we think we sound.

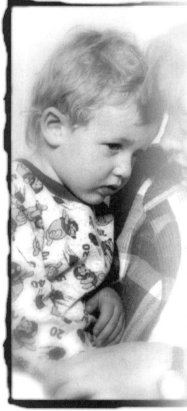

Encourage prayer as a habit of conversation with God. People who endured terrible situations say they survived them because they knew God was with them. You want your child to have this same kind of security, this conviction that God is close at all times. No matter how difficult our circumstances, God is present with us like a best friend. Even better, God never tires of us. God always wants to hear whatever we want to say. (This includes even our anger or frustration. The Hebrew psalms are full of rage, because people who are close to God know they can trust God with any emotion they are feeling.)

To instill a habit of prayer as conversation with a good and ever-present God is a great gift to your child. It will carry him or her through both joys and sadnesses that we cannot predict. Our children will surely encounter experiences that are too much for them to explain or endure from a human viewpoint. They will need to turn, often and trustingly, to God. Later, as an adult who continues this nurturing habit of conversational prayer, your child will look back and thank you for planting the seeds so early in life.

You may want to begin by teaching your child several of the prayers found in the appendix at the back of this book (p. 150). But at the same time, remind your child that we can always talk with God in our own words. Alternate spontaneous prayer with more formal prayers, so that your child can use both languages with ease.

As family expert Dolores Curran points out, some abstractions in the Hail Mary or Our Father may puzzle young children. Her advice, "Don't avoid them, but don't dwell on them either." Say, "'thy will be done' means that whatever God wants, you will do, or that 'fruit of thy womb' means baby."[3]

For more resources on formal prayer, check your local bookstore, a website for books, or ask your catechist. Remember that your becoming a prayerful person is a powerful model for your child. If you value prayer enough to make time for it in a busy schedule, so will your child.

Bedtime Prayer

A peaceful way to end each day is by reviewing its events. Some people call this "PJ Time" (a fuller account may be found in *Sleeping with Bread* by Dennis, Matthew and Sheila Linn). It is based on the idea that God is constantly active in our everyday experience. God continues to be present in *our* stories, doing the same things we find God doing in the Bible. The sooner we become alert and sensitive to that process, the better we will become at recognizing and responding to it. Children who learn to trust their own inner wisdom will be more centered as adults, more confident in their decisions. Furthermore, whatever we dwell on while awake can also enter the unconscious. If, as children and as adults we fall asleep saying "thank you," we can sleep with grateful hearts.[4]

You may start this nighttime reflection by having everyone in the family answer simple questions like, "What was best about your day? Worst?" or "When were you happiest? Saddest?" With older children, you might ask, "Where were you closest to God? Furthest away?" During this time some people ask each other for forgiveness of the little hurts that creep into every family's life.

One mom confided that she and her husband lay their hands gently on their children's foreheads after they're asleep. They pray for the "healing of memories," any hurts they may not know about, especially those they may have caused.

Another mother recounts a conversation with her eight-year-old son as he drifted off to sleep. Erik mused, "I wonder if this is normal. I feel this irritating longing inside. I have a sense that something isn't finished."

The mother replied, "Keep track of that. It's important not to fill up the hole with junk."

"OK," said Erik. "Goodnight."

His mother later told a friend, "I hope he can stay open and empty to that longing for mystery, not try to fill it up with plastic stuff from the mall that will never satisfy his deepest yearning."

Seasonal Prayer

In addition to prayer based on the sacramental symbols, introduce simple rituals based on the seasons of the liturgical year. For Christians, the life of Christ is the template placed over our lives to give them meaning and direction. Beginning in Advent (the start of the liturgical year), the readings follow Christ's life from his conception to his birth (Christmas), childhood, baptism, public life, to his passion and death during Lent, and his rising at Easter and coming to new life through his church at Pentecost.

By celebrating the liturgical seasons in our homes, we help children to appreciate their flow and become familiar with the Christian story, absorbing its meaning as naturally as the knowledge that we wear heavy clothes in winter and lighter ones in summer. Some seasonal celebrations follow:

Seasonal Celebrations

Late Nov., early Dec.
Advent

Make an Advent wreath out of evergreen boughs tied in a circle. Light one candle during each of the four weeks leading up to Christmas. Advent calendars and Jesse trees are also ways to celebrate—ask your parish leader for directions.

December 6
Feast of St. Nicholas

Parents can fill children's shoes, left outside their doors, with candy and small gifts. Children can become little Nicholases, doing secret kindnesses for others.

December 12
Feast of Our Lady of Guadalupe

Make some colorful flowers out of construction paper to honor Mary in her role as the patron of all the Americas.

December 24
Christmas Eve

Have a special creche made out of sturdy figures that small fingers can't break. Create family traditions around special foods, ethnic customs, music or stories that celebrate Christmas.

January 6
Epiphany

Celebrate the coming of the kings to visit Jesus by blessing your home or writing on the door in chalk the year and the initials of the traditional names of the three kings (Caspar, Melchior, Balthasar).

February 2
Presentation of the Lord

The gospel (Luke 2:22-40) for this feast proclaims that the child Jesus is a light for all peoples. Celebrate the light your child has brought into your life, by lighting several candles and praying with them, as suggested on p. 82.

Last Tuesday before Lent
Mardi Gras

Celebrated in New Orleans with feasts and parades, you can plan a special desert and decorate a wagon or tricycle for a float. This is the last party before Lent begins.

First Day of Lent
Ash Wednesday

The ashes marked on our foreheads mean that we are dust, and to dust we shall return. Such a mystery cannot be explained in words; we rely on the symbol to carry profound meaning.

March 17
Feast of St. Patrick

Tell or read your child the story to explain why we wear green in honor of the feast. Honor other ethnic heroes on their feast days too.

March 19
Feast of St. Joseph

Replicate the Italian custom of St. Joseph's table, on which the people of a parish would set out bread and other food for the poor. Introduce your family to a wide variety of breads from many cultures: pita, scones, croissants, German rye, Irish soda bread, Indian fry bread, challah, tortillas, etc. Donate some to a local food bank for the poor and enjoy some yourself.

March 25
Feast of the Annunciation

Tell or read your child the story of the angel bringing good news to Mary that she

Seasonal Celebrations

would have a baby named Jesus (Luke 1:26-38).

Sunday before Easter
Passion or Palm Sunday

Many families make crosses out of the palms distributed at church. Show your child how to cut a small slit and slip one piece through perpendicular to the other.

Holy Week
The Sacred Three Days (Triduum)

Holy Thursday
Good Friday
Holy Saturday

Check with your parish about appropriate activities for children or suggestions for celebrating this week in your home.

Easter Sunday
Feast of Our Lord's Resurrection

Decorate Easter eggs, an Easter candle or an Easter tree with your child. The tree can be a bare bough on which you hang home-made ornaments, such as cut-outs of flowers, birds and butterflies. You may also make figures such as angels from pipe cleaners or buy egg ornaments in craft stores.

March 31
Feast of the Visitation

Tell or read your child the story of Mary's visit to her cousin Elizabeth when they were both pregnant (Luke 1:39-56). Listen to a musical version of Mary's song, the "Magnificat."

Fifty Days after Easter
Pentecost

Wear red to celebrate the coming of the Spirit in tongues of fire. Eat strawberries; decorate with red flowers. Listen to or sing a hymn asking the Holy Spirit to fill our lives with love.

June 24
Feast of John the Baptist

Tell again this story of Jesus' cousin and herald who ate locusts and honey (Matthew 3:1-17).

August 15
Feast of Mary's Assumption into Heaven

Many communities celebrate Mary's being taken bodily into heaven with harvest feasts. In many countries, this is the time to bless fields and crops. Make a vegetable or fruit dish for breakfast or dinner; decorate the table with flowers and fruits.

November 1
Feast of All Saints

Display pictures of all the "saints"—canonized or not—who grace our lives. Invite the children to include pictures of their teachers, friends, grandparents, etc.

November 2
Feast of All Souls

Display pictures of those who have died but who still bring meaning and blessing into our lives. Light a candle to honor them. Or go through the family album and tell stories about the pictures.

November
Thanksgiving

During the month of November, ask family members to name one thing they are grateful for each day. By the time you finally reach Thanksgiving, you may have a fuller appreciation of all you've been given.

Patron Saint or Feast Days

Many children enjoy celebrating the feast of the saint for whom they are named. This doesn't mean adding on another day that must be prefaced by time-consuming shopping trips or lengthy cooking sessions. Who needs more stress? Instead, prepare the child's favorite meal, or make a simple crown from construction paper. The biggest treat for some children is simply to have a parent spend time with them alone, going for a walk, chatting, admiring the sunset, breaking out of routines. Read a book about the saint, or gradually introduce your child to others of the same name who have been heroes, said wise things, or contributed to humanity in some way. One family collected a box of perfect skipping rocks for their son's feast day. Of course they celebrated by going to a nearby pond and trying them out!

My child's feast day is:

Our way to celebrate it is:

At age 2

At age 3

At age 4

At age 5

At age 6

Looking toward First Eucharist:
Prayer with Bread and Wine

As your child draws near to the celebration of first eucharist, your prayer together may focus on eucharistic themes. Review together some of the responses of the Mass, which your child may already know from celebrating eucharist with you.

The Lord be with you.
And also with you.

The Word of the Lord.
Thanks be to God.

The gospel of the Lord.
Praise to you, Lord Jesus Christ.

Christ has died,
Christ is risen,
Christ will come again.

Lift up your hearts.
We lift them up to the Lord.

Let us give thanks to the Lord our God.
It is right to give God thanks and praise.

The peace of the Lord be with you.
And also with you.

Practice setting a small table at your child's height with a cloth, crucifix, candles, cup and plate. Show how the table we set for meals at home is like the table at church where we share Christ's meal. Exchange a sign of peace—a handshake or a hug. Share a little bread and wine or grape juice (explaining that it is practice, not the real eucharist). Read or tell the story of Jesus' last supper with his friends, emphasizing his words:

> Take this, all of you, and eat it:
> This is my body which will be given up for you.

> Take this, all of you, and drink from it:
> this is the cup of my blood...
> Do this in memory of me.

Sing a verse or the chorus of eucharistic hymns used in your parish, having your child choose favorites.

Make a small loaf of bread and a cup of wine or grape juice your focal point as you talk about how Jesus gave us himself in bread and wine. Ask your child to remember a favorite meal, perhaps for a birthday or holiday. Who came? Why was it special? Record the answers or draw a picture of the meal here:

Then show how the eucharist is like our favorite meal, because we gather with friends, we hear stories, we thank, we sing, we eat and drink. Most especially, Jesus gives us the gift of himself in the blessed bread and wine that we receive at Mass.

The word *eucharist* means thanks. Join in a prayer of thanksgiving out loud, perhaps around a dining table, where you and your child and other family members take turns thanking God for God's gifts.

Use a blessing cup as a family ritual at mealtimes. Choose a special glass or goblet and fill it with milk or juice. Each member of the family says a simple prayer, drinks from the cup and passes it on to the next person. You may want to do this on important days like anniversaries, birthdays, when a guest is present, or for the first day of school or summer vacation. Examples of spontaneous prayers as you pass it around are:

> Thank you for the spaghetti dinner.
> Bless Luke on his birthday.
> Please help Grandma get over the flu.
> Be with the people of Japan, who just had the
>   earthquake.

As you and your child look forward to first communion, what are you most grateful for? Write or draw responses in the space on the next page.

We Are Grateful for...

Notes
1. Jerome W. Berryman, "The Young Child and Scripture," in
   Beginning the Journey: From Infant Baptism to First Eucharist
   (Washington, DC: U.S. Catholic Conference, 1994), 55.
2. Sofia Cavalletti, *The Religious Potential of the Child* (New York: Paulist Press, 1983), 102.
3. Dolores Curran, *On Family Prayer* (Mystic, CT: Twenty-Third Publications, 1997), 10.
4. Dennis, Sheila and Matthew Linn, *Sleeping with Bread* (New York: Paulist Press, 1995),
   10-11.

For the very young child, snuggling in bed with a parent reading aloud *The Runaway Bunny* or *Goodnight Moon* can be a sacrament of love and trust.

Chapter 4

Storytelling and Scripture

Personal Stories

"Tell me a story!" You may often hear this plea from your child. What's behind it? There may be more to it than you might at first think. Almost everyone is drawn to stories because we want to know how they end, to live the lives of other people, to share vicariously in the characters' joys and tragedies and to experience the dynamic pattern of beginning, middle and end. The child's wish for a story may show a longing for meaning, for security, for the soothing sound of a parent's voice to hold at bay the goblins of the night. "We listen to stories and we read them because we are searching for paradigms into which our own story will fit."[1] We see ourselves as actors in our own stories, and children especially want to be the brave hero or courageous heroine.

How do we make sense of our own stories? We have all felt at times our own smallness—we stand under a star-filled sky or beside the ocean and realize how tiny one individual seems in the vast scheme of things. By linking our "small s" stories with the "capital S" story of Jesus, our joys gain depth and substance; our suffering takes on meaning. We realize that it is not just about us—we are part of a grander, larger design. We and our children are linked to ancestors who came before and descendants who will come after us in a mysterious process that began long before our births and will continue long after our deaths.

We are not alone and we are not unimportant. All of us want to give our children a sense of meaning, a sense of their own dignity. We want them to have the kind of inner security that will not be swayed by the latest fad or the strongest peer pressure.

Surprisingly, that centered self-image may not come from reading the latest child development theory or learning the best parenting techniques. While such tools are helpful, they often overlook what is closer to hand: the direct, immediate stuff of our own experience.

What is true for individuals is also true for families. According to Mary Pipher, "stories reveal what a family wants to believe about itself."[2] Certain stories become so central to the family's repertoire that even though everyone groans when they begin, no one would ever interfere with the proper telling. These stories reveal who the family heroes are, how the family survives disasters and what the family values most. Sometimes the stories are embarrassing, but they teach us that we can laugh at ourselves and that an experience which once seemed like the ultimate humiliation can, with the perspective of time, become funny. Children raised in a rich context of story know their identity, history and philosophy in concrete, direct ways.

In the space below, recount briefly a significant family story from your childhood. Use this sentence to get started. "Remember the time we..."

You may have listened to the story told above so often you groaned every time you heard it coming. But you would never want to lose it. Why do you think it was so important to your growing up? What did it tell you about your family or yourself?

Both the Davidson study done at Purdue University and the Search Institute study that sought to discover the most important factors contributing to mature faith concluded that hearing their parents' faith stories is one of the most important influences on the faith of children and teenagers.

What story from your family of origin do you most want to tell your child?

What story of a personal struggle might help your child as he or she matures and deals with similar issues?

Faith Stories

Everything that is true about family stories is also true for the stories cherished by the community of faith. Our sacred stories tell us of brave, cunning, compassionate ancestors in faith like Abraham, Noah, Sarah, Esther, Solomon, David, Judith, the Samaritan woman, Peter, Martha, Thomas, Mary Magdalene, Catherine of Siena, Teresa of Avila, Thomas More, Oscar Romero, Dorothy Day. They tell us that we can be more: we can be like the saints.

Not only do they hold up models; they describe the relationship that makes it all possible. Over and over the Bible tells us of a God who cherishes a people even though they are stupid, selfish and stubborn. The unbounded love of the covenant relationship is also offered to us, no matter how often we fail or how repeatedly we stumble.

What is your favorite Bible story?

What does this choice of scripture tell you about yourself?

It All Began with Story

When you think of Christianity's beginnings, what comes to mind first? It all started with a little band of folks telling stories of Jesus—his wondrous healings, his own parable stories, his death and rising. Everything else—dogmas, creeds, theology, laws—came later. Jerome Berryman imagines the first telling of these stories around the fire at night, with children snuggled close to their parents. "The stories wrapped the children in meaning and protected them like blankets against the cold and chaos of the night."[3]

These stories can still enfold our children in meaning. Before a child reads, he or she has a sensitivity to language unmatched in later life. This is the reason why children absorb, apparently with little effort, the whole complex grammar and structure of a language by the time they are three years old. Pre-reading children are also adept at learning foreign languages; experts agree that the early years are the best time to learn a second language.

But there are more than academic reasons to read aloud with children, to share stories around a campfire, at the kitchen table or in the car. Stories can "clarify the truth, offer opportunities to laugh and cry, awaken spiritual awareness, heal wounds, build memory banks, and unite communities."[4] Without stories, "propositions about faith are dull and lifeless."[5] For the very young child, snuggling in bed with a parent reading aloud *The Runaway Bunny* or *Goodnight Moon* can be a sacrament of love and trust.

This sensitivity of young children also makes early childhood an ideal time to hear Bible stories. Waiting until the third or fourth grade is too late: "If we miss the early years, we miss grounding Scripture as the child's own family story."[6] The Bible gives us a collection of ancestors that are both human in their failings and brilliant for their bravery or kindness.

Notice how often Jesus tells a story when he wants to get a point across. His teaching setting was a tough one—not the hushed, respectful quiet of a classroom, but the noisy, rowdy marketplace, the road, or the home where many other events competed for people's attention. He knew that listing rules or proclaiming laws would fail to snag his listeners, so he told stories. Often these "upset the apple cart," or concluded with a "zinger" ending. Two thousand years later, despite multiple distractions, they can still capture our attention, upset our cherished assumptions and zing us with their point.

Storytelling in early childhood also begins a process of "landscaping the religious imagination." Paul Philibert points out that using our imaginations we create the "deep structure" of our world's meaning. These images are more important than logic or words and give us a sense of being unique individuals. Advertising media, bypassing rational faculties, skillfully uses images to influence us to buy objects that enhance self-image.

"Some of our most enduring symbols are formed in the earliest years of life" as we relate to our parents and "come to belong to the story of Jesus."[7] Children's personal moments of coming close to God then become part of the inner narrative that shapes the direction of their lives. "When children's eyes become large as saucers while listening to the old stories, they reveal for us the power of story and rite to transform hearts."[8]

Practical Tips for Storytelling

- Start with your own favorite stories—those of heroes like Joshua, Judith, Moses or Miriam. Or perhaps you prefer the tender, quiet stories of the Annunciation, Nativity or the wondrous sharing of loaves and fishes to the clash and drama of battle and sword. You may want to focus on stories that show how God cared for people long ago, perhaps the story of God's providing bread to eat (manna) and water from a rock as the Hebrew people wandered in the desert after leaving Egypt. Or tell of Jesus' kindness, for example when he awakened a little girl who had died and told her parents to get her something to eat (Luke 8:49-56).

- Time is short, so choose the stories that will speak to your child's heart and be solidly comforting. Choose the stories that focus on God's love; reserve for later those you struggle with.
- Singing to calm a crying infant can convey the peace of Christ. A simple refrain like "Jesus, friend" won't necessarily quiet the baby, but it will soothe the parent!
- Children love action and movement, so whenever possible incorporate it into your storytelling. Change your voice for different characters in the story. (The techniques that work for "The Three Bears" also apply to Bible stories.)
  — Act out stories with dolls, puppets, or a handkerchief knotted to look like a human figure. Several possibilities appear below.

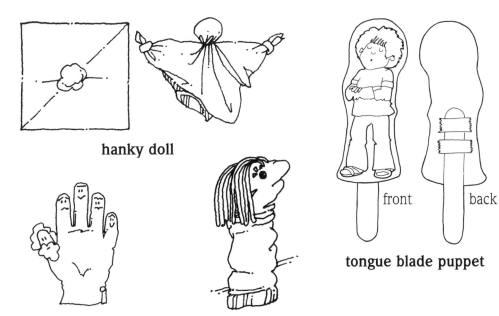

hanky doll

glove finger puppets

sock puppet

tongue blade puppet

front   back

— For the Nativity story, your child can rock a (doll) baby Jesus and sing him a lullaby.

— The child can retell his own version of favorite tales with figures made from wood, popsicle sticks or cottonballs. Parent and child together can create props, using their imaginations.

— Play "sheep and shepherd" by having your child hide, and the parent, on hands and knees, go look for her. "Here's my sweetie!" mom or dad cheers. And the child snuggles into the great security of being found.

— Have a picnic on the living room floor as you read the story about Jesus feeding 5,000. It need not be an elaborate meal. Water in a teacup with a cracker is enough if it's shared with a parent and lots of laughter.

— As you tell the story of Jesus taking the children in his arms, reinforce the message of unconditional love by taking your child in your arms, saying, "Jesus loves you just the way you are. And so do I."

• Keep a family Bible in a special place in the house. Your children will pick up on your respect for this unique book that helps us make sense of our lives. Also find a well illustrated children's Bible, or Bible stories illustrated by artists like Brian Wildsmith or Tomie DePaola (see Appendix, p. 157). You can also create your own book of favorite family stories or Bible stories, following this simple procedure. Fold several large pieces of blank paper in half. Make a slightly larger cover from a piece of construction paper. Staple or tie together with yarn. Add a title on the cover. (See diagram on next page.)

- Make connections between your child's experiences and Bible stories. If the family or preschool goes on a picnic, remember how Jesus once had a picnic when he showed his friends where to catch fish, then barbecued some for them! Or when we argue with a sibling—recall how Jesus once told a story about two brothers. The younger one ran off and spent all the money; the older one complained about the party celebrating his return. If we grow a beautiful melon vine in the backyard or ivy on the house, tell how Jesus once talked about our relationship with him in terms of a vine and branches. When we eat a meal together, remind your child that Jesus did that often, and had a special last supper when he had to tell his friends goodbye.

- Making a Jesse tree is a fine way to tell the stories of Jesus' great-great-grandparents. During Advent, hang a symbol for each person on a bare branch. Even if you add one a year and save it, you will have a good start on a collection by the time your child enters grade school.

Using these diagrams as a guide, create Jesse tree ornaments. Enlarge and duplicate these or create your own. Mount on felt or construction paper and hang with thread or yarn on the bare branches..

Jesse

Creation

Adam and Eve

Noah

Abraham

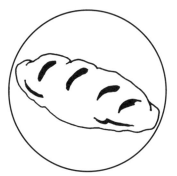

Sarah

Isaac

Jacob

Joseph

Moses   Miriam   Mary

Joshua   Rahab   Ruth

- Remember that strong Christian messages are often presented in books that are not necessarily "religious." The classics of children's literature give a child security and assurance, the grounding in trust that forms the basis for a life of faith.
- One of the most important parts of parenting is becoming a good storyteller. Attend workshops on this art at your parish or local school if they are offered; get good books; become friendly with your children's librarian; find out when bookstores or libraries offer story hour.

Use the space below to record your child's favorite books or stories.

At age 2

At age 3

At age 4

At age 5

At age 6

Notes

1. Andrew Greeley and Mary Durkin, *How to Save the Catholic Church* (New York: Viking, 1984), 83.
2. Mary Pipher, *The Shelter of Each Other* (New York: Ballantine, 1996), 244.
3. Jerome Berryman, "The Young Child and Scripture," in *Beginning the Journey: From Infant Baptism to First Eucharist* (Washington, DC: United States Catholic Conference), 50.
4. Janaan Manternach, "Stories Tell of Transformation and Are Transforming," *Faithworks*, August/September 1999, 3.
5. Maureen Gallagher, *The Art of Catechesis* (New York: Paulist Press, 1998), 75-89.
6. Berryman, "The Young Child and Scripture," 51.
7. Paul Philibert, "Landscaping the Religious Imagination," in Eleanor Bernstein and John Brooks-Leonard, eds., *Children in the Assembly of the Church* (Chicago: Liturgy Training Publications, 1992), 17, 20.
8. Ibid., 27.

If I had influence with the good fairy
who is supposed to preside over the
christening of all children, I should ask
that her gift to each child in the world be
a sense of wonder so indestructible that
it would last throughout life.

—*Rachel Carson*

Chapter 5

Children and Nature

Parents have the unique privilege of introducing children to a marvelously colored, beautiful, varied world. A parent's emotion is contagious—whether it is enthusiasm for a brook trout in a rushing stream, serenity in a snowy field, awe before a waterfall, or pride in homegrown tomatoes. A parent's excitement can convince a child that a walk through the woods is a great adventure. "One of the greatest gifts parents can give their children is to teach them to love the natural world."[1]

Think back on your own childhood. Record here an experience of nature that you remember vividly.

A woman who has been active in campus ministry and teaching religion most of her adult life remembers how her dad, an Iowa farmer, sowed the seeds of faith in her life. "All my religious upbringing goes back to our walks through the fields. He would crumble a grain of wheat in his hands or listen to a brook with such *reverence*. His attitude taught me to see signs everywhere that God is with us, that the world is a good place, that we're going to be OK."

Most parents would probably agree that they want their children to see the world as permeated by grace, to know we are always in the presence of God, to find a deep security and source of healing no further than their own backyard. So we sow the seeds early, taking care to create in the youngest child a sure sense that being outdoors is a good place to be. Giving children an appreciation of nature isn't limited to those living in rural areas. Urban families can still enjoy the community gardens, parks, back yards, patios, lakes, rivers and fountains of the city. Rachel Carson once described this precious gift to children:

> If I had influence with the good fairy who is supposed to preside over the christening of all children, I should ask that her gift to each child in the world be a sense of wonder so indestructible that it would last throughout life, as an unfailing antidote against boredom and disenchantments of later years, the sterile preoccupation with things that are artificial, the alienation from the sources of our strength....
>
> Those who dwell, as scientists or laity, among the beauties and mysteries of the earth are never alone or weary of life. Whatever the vexations or concerns of their personal lives, their thoughts can find paths that lead to inner contentment and to renewed excitement in living. Those who contemplate the beauty of the earth find reserves of strength that will endure as long as life lasts.[2]

We know that children need 'wild' places.[3] Look back at the memory of nature that you recalled earlier, but this time go beyond description to analysis. What did your experience of nature give you? Did it bring a sense of security, comfort from a crazy world or angry voices? Did it impress you with its power, increasing your sense of smallness and vulnerability? Were you able to simply sink into beauty and forget time for a while? What did it bring?

Research on young children reveals that "a child's sense of identity often is supported by small, intimate places rather than large, expansive ones. While we as adults often tend toward the panoramic view, children look at the details of things."[4] For this reason, children may often create a "nest" under a bush or build an enclosure from the pillows of the couch. They like to make "tents" with blankets or burrow beneath a bed.

Their fascination with tiny things extends to every bug they can discover. A walk that might take an adult ten minutes will take a child an hour because he or she

must pause to examine every twig, snail, pebble, leaf and feather along the way. Furthermore, a child's propensity to collect small objects can quickly drive a parent crazy. But these possessions are important for they are the beginning of a relationship with the natural world and of a rootedness that will long outlast the collection itself.

Watch a two-year-old running dirt between her fingers or turning a bug over in his hand. A child is directly, uncompromisingly "in" a body—even more so before language and reading skills develop. Clearly, that child is meant to be in direct, physical relationship with the world through all the senses. We look to the natural world, not to television or video games, for that experience. Few other cultures are as removed from the natural world as we are. To reclaim our connections, we not only make field trips with our children to zoos and aquariums, but we can also discover a world in a small plot of the backyard, a pot of soil indoors, or a neighboring park.

Rachel Carson describes a night when she wrapped her twenty-month-old nephew in a blanket and took him outside to hear the roar of waves and appreciate the stars overhead. "Together we laughed for pure joy—he a baby meeting for the first time the wild tumult of Oceanus, I with the salt of half a lifetime of sea love in me. But I think we felt the same spine-tingling response to the vast, roaring ocean and the wild night around us."[5]

She encourages parents who feel they know little nature lore to realize that they can still do much for their child.

Among her suggestions: looking at the stars, listening to the wind, feeling rain on the face, watching the birds' migrations and noticing the changing seasons.

Tell here of a time you and your child appreciated nature together. What did you see? hear? touch? taste? smell?

Have your child draw an experience of nature or a time outdoors. Or tape in a feather, a dried flower or a leaf that he has found, that is special to her.

My Time Outdoors

From caring for animals, children learn responsibility. Through their pets they can experience the realities of birth and death that once occurred in homes but are now tucked away in hospitals. A six-year-old living in rural Missouri midwifed goats, and five months later was present when a baby goat named Sylvie died. As he held Sylvie he reassured her, "You're going someplace good. But you'll have to let go of me to go there." Finally, he held her up and said, "Go to God." It seems safe to say that a child with such a profound understanding of death will become an adult who isn't nervous around such realities and can empathize with people who are dying.

Our children will grow up in a world increasingly conscious of ecology. In the elementary grades, they will learn about the interconnected web of life and how to protect the marvels of soil, ocean and air.

Record here your child's experiences of nature. Does he or she seem especially drawn to water—in lakes, rivers, rain, puddles, or oceans? to sky—during the day or at night? to flowers or plants? to animals? to hills, shores, rocks or mountains? to fire or wind? Recording that attraction here could do your child a great service later in life; he or she will then know where to find the sources of strength.

At age 2:

At age 3:

At age 4:

At age 5:

At age 6:

Does your child have a favorite place outside? Describe it.

What natural objects does your child like to collect?

Thomas Merton once said, "It is essential to experience all the times and moods of one good place."[6] That takes a lot of stillness, but it is worth the effort to spend quiet time, absorbing the fullness of summer or the changes of seasons, the shadows on the lake or the hillside, the different colors of leaves in April or October.

Nature and the Creator

Nature also tells us about God who created it. The beauty, infinite variety, and power we find in the world tell us of the personality of the Creator just as surely as a friend's art work tells us something of her personality. For many people, a natural setting is often a better place for prayer than a church. Sister Joyce Rupp writes of struggling for years with the common teaching that her prayer and "major spiritual impetus should especially be with the Scriptures, with the Eucharist, and with my relationships." While she occasionally met God there, she never had the intense, mystical experiences she had when she spent time with the earth. "Anytime I was with the earth in a contemplative mode, I found a taste of honey for my soul."[7] She reached this conclusion in her forties; but now children don't have to wait quite so long.

For centuries, creation has prompted prayers of praise. The Psalmist writes,

> Those who live at earth's farthest bounds are awed
>   by your signs;
> you make the gateways of the morning and the
>   evening shout for joy.

You visit the earth and water it, you greatly enrich it;
the river of God is full of water;
you provide the people with grain, for so you have
    prepared it.
You water its furrows abundantly, settling its ridges,
softening it with showers, and blessing its growth.
You crown the year with your bounty;
your wagon tracks overflow with richness.
The pastures of the wilderness overflow,
the hills gird themselves with joy,
the meadows clothe themselves with flocks,
the valleys deck themselves with grain,
they shout and sing together for joy (65:8-13).

The floods have lifted up, O LORD,
the floods have lifted up their voice;
the floods lift up their roaring.
More majestic than the thunders of mighty waters,
more majestic than the waves of the sea,
majestic on high is the LORD! (93:3-4).

Let the heavens be glad, and let the earth rejoice;
let the sea roar, and all that fills it;
let the field exult, and everything in it.
Then shall all the trees of the forest sing for joy
before the LORD; ... (96:11-12).

Jesus was clearly drawn to the beauty of creation: he drew
on elements of the natural world, like vineyards, birds,
sheep, flowers and water to convey his message. For him,
lilies represented not only God's beauty but also God's

sustaining care. "Consider the lilies of the field, how they grow; they neither toil nor spin, yet I tell you, even Solomon in all his glory was not clothed like one of these. But if God so clothes the grass of the field, which is alive today and tomorrow is thrown into the oven, will he not much more clothe you—you of little faith?" (Mt. 6:28-30).

St. Augustine wrote,

> "Question the beauty of the earth, question the beauty of the sea, question the beauty of the air...question the beauty of the sky...question all these realities. All respond: 'See, we are beautiful.' Their beauty is a profession. These beauties are subject to change. Who made them if not the Beautiful One who is not subject to change?" (quoted in the *Catechism of the Catholic Church*, #32)

The beauty we admire in church is but a small slice of the larger, natural world in which we find God reflected. The Church uses natural elements that represent the larger world of God's creation. So the beauty of candlelight, song, incense, stained glass, gold, wood and linen direct us back toward the play of sunlight and shadow, the song of bird or cascade, the solidity of mountain, rock or tree trunk. No artifice veils nature. There we can find something of substance that is not tawdry, or deprived of its original innocence. Then we join with Jesuit poet Gerard Manley Hopkins in saying, "The world is charged with the grandeur of God."

Has the beauty or power of creation led you to any insights about the Creator? If so, describe these.

Activities with Nature

Make a "treasure box" by decorating a shoe box or empty coffee can. This then becomes the place for your child to keep special objects he or she has found outdoors—the pebbles, shells, etc. that might otherwise decorate the whole house!

One thing kids will almost certainly eat is a vegetable they have grown themselves. Have them plant their favorites (carrots, lettuce, snow peas, radishes, beans, etc.), watch the seeds sprout, weed and water them. If you do not have much yard space, check on what can be grown indoors or in a pot on a patio, balcony or deck. At the end of this process your child can enjoy fresh tastes as well as the pride of accomplishment.

What can we learn from nature? Try this exercise in birth and rebirth. If your child has grown some plants, let one of them go to seed. Save the seed, an elemental gift of God. Imagine what it means for a family whose whole livelihood depends on it. Then plant it the following year. Without saying a word on the topic, you will have taught your child an unforgettable lesson about birth, death and rebirth. The natural cycle often says more than our words can. It's the same with planting bulbs. That dull brown, crusty lump we plant in the fall becomes a fragrant hyacinth or a brilliant daffodil in spring. A child who experiences that transformation first-hand already knows a great deal about the Christian mystery of death and resurrection.

Next time you need a greeting card, make one with your child. Most grandparents and many friends will cherish that creative expression far longer than they would an anonymous commercial product. All it takes are crayons, paints or markers, construction paper or card stock and, for more elaborate projects, scissors, glue and ribbon. Try to incorporate dried grasses, leaves or flowers that your child has found outdoors.

Using the psalms above or your own favorites as a model, write your own version of a psalm of praise, with children helping to describe the natural things for which they want to praise the Creator.

Adopt a tree, or plant one to honor your child's birth date. Then record its changes or mark its growth, perhaps by measuring your child's height against it annually. Or take pictures of the tree from the same angle in all four seasons, noting the changes in the leaves.

Celebrate the change of seasons with simple annual rituals: a picnic beneath fall leaves, hot cocoa for the first snowfall, a "discovery" walk to find the first signs of spring, a swim on the first hot summer day. Your imagination and the area in which you live will determine more specifically what you do.

Help your child learn simple prayers based on the psalms that celebrate some of the things he or she also likes. (While the child may not fully comprehend the meaning, he or she will still like the mystery and beauty of the lines. Furthermore, the lines will create pictures in the imagination far more beautiful than any advertising jingle or image created by television.) The following psalm verses are taken from the American Bible Society's *The Holy Bible: Contemporary English Version,* which is recommended for use in Masses for children.

> The heavens keep telling the wonders of God,
> and the skies declare what God has done (19:1).

> The voice of the LORD echoes over the oceans.
> The glorious LORD God thunders
> above the roar of the raging sea (29:3).

> Good people will prosper like palm trees,
> and they will grow strong like the cedars of Lebanon
>   (92:12).

> God created us, and we belong to God;
> we are God's people, the sheep of God's pasture
>   (100:3).

The mountains and the hills skipped around like goats...
Ask the mountains and the hills why they skipped like
    goats! (114:4, 6).

The Lord is your protector, and he won't go to sleep
    or let you stumble.
The protector of Israel doesn't doze or even get
    drowsy (121:5-6).

Suppose I had wings like the dawning day
    and flew across the ocean.
Even then your powerful arm
    would guide and protect me.
Or suppose I said, "I'll hide in the dark
    until night comes to cover me over."
But you see in the dark
because daylight and dark
    are all the same to you (139:9-12).

Notes

1. Mary Pipher, *The Shelter of Each Other*
   (New York: Ballantine, 1996), 234.
2. Rachel Carson, *The Sense of Wonder*
   (New York: Harper and Row, 1956), 42-43, 88.
3. Robert Hamma, *Landscapes of the Soul* (Notre Dame:
   Ave Maria Press, 1999), 92.
4. Ibid., 97.
5. Carson, *The Sense of Wonder*, 9.
6. Thomas Merton, *Conjectures of a Guilty Bystander*
   (Garden City, NY: Image Books, 1968), 179.
7. Joyce Rupp, *Dear Heart, Come Home* (New York:
   Crossroad, 1996), 125, 92.

You prepare children for the eucharistic
table through the meals you share
throughout their childhoods.

Chapter 6

Looking toward First Eucharist

In the space below, describe a favorite meal; perhaps a holiday celebration at home or a meal shared with a friend or spouse at a special restaurant. What did you eat? What was the setting?

If you have remembered this meal more than all the others you have eaten, it must have had some ingredients more important than the food. What do you remember about:

the conversation?

the companion(s)?

the emotions felt or expressed?

When we eat alone or on the run, we may receive the same caloric content to energize the body. But something is missing. The soul is not fed; the spirit starves.

No parent would ever knowingly and willingly let a child starve. Conscientiously and regularly, we provide our children with physical food. We'd feel terrible if we couldn't. But how well do we feed them spiritually?

That's what the eucharist is all about. It is a source of nurture that we definitely want to pass on to our children: a bread that is more than bread and wine that is more than wine. Some people call it "food for the journey." What more could we ask than that Jesus nurture us with his own body and blood? How much more intimate could we become with him? How could we draw any closer to this source of our eternal life?

One day just after communion, a man who'd struggled with doubt realized, "'This is all I will ever need.' This faith. This God. This Jesus."[1] We may dismiss this easily but, if we think about it, has not such an attitude sustained the saints and martyrs? It helps explain why sometimes people who have relinquished a great deal still have deep joy. They may have had to surrender health, loved ones, finances or homes. But they have what is important, an abundant source of nurture for adults as well as children.

Background for Eucharist: The Domestic Table

You prepare children for the eucharistic table through the meals you share throughout their childhoods. Children know that at the kitchen table, they are fed with more than food; they also crave the companionship and sharing that accompanies most meals. The dilemma for many families is that while they may want to eat together, they cannot find the time for it. Too many activities crowd into the dinner hour, and various family members have different responsibilities that take them away at this time. Rather than feel guilty about missed mealtimes, some families deal creatively with the time crunch and devise strategies to make shared meals a priority.

One strategy is to explore the possibilities for shared meals other than dinner. If one parent is always working or one child always has soccer practice then, what about breakfast or a late evening snack when everyone is home? No one is saying that someone in the family must produce a four-course meal; a bagel split in the early morning or a bowl of popcorn before bed might capture some of the same warm feelings around the sharing of food. And no matter how crazy the schedule, most families can find at least one time (perhaps during the weekend) for a special shared meal. Remember that all the work need not fall on one set of shoulders; even the youngest children can help with table-setting, potato-peeling or bread-buttering.

Some families who feel stressed by their schedules are restoring a sense of "Sabbath," a time of rest that may fall on Sunday but could be another day as well. We who feel overworked can empathize with the repetition in the passage that tells of Sabbath origins:

> And on the seventh day God finished the work that he had done, and he rested on the seventh day from all the work that he had done. So God blessed the seventh day and hallowed it, because on it God rested from all the work that he had done in creation (Genesis 2:2-4).

God apparently worked hard too. Then God took a breather.

We work hard so that someday all life will look like Sabbath; all other days are for the sake of Sabbath. In the Jewish tradition, people stopped what they were doing to place limits and boundaries on work. They took out the beautiful tablecloth, baked the special bread, made love with their spouses, laid hands on their children's heads in gratitude and blessing. For practical ways to adopt Sabbath customs today, see Wayne Muller's *Sabbath.*

Some faith communities continue the last custom during a Sunday service. They call forth the children, bless them, name God's love for them, vow to the children and each other that they will do all they can to help them grow up safely. In a dangerous world, it reassures children about their security.

The child who is grounded in years of shared mealtimes knows the message underlying the meal. Someone (mom, dad, grandma, an older sibling or whoever cooked) loved them enough to sacrifice time and energy to prepare this meal. As one dad writes:

> When I make lunches for my girls, I focus on this: The sandwiches are sacraments. Not the miracle of transubstantiation, but certainly parallel with it, moving in the same direction. If I could give my children my body to eat, again and again without losing it, my body like the loaves and fishes going endlessly into mouths and stomachs, I would do it.[2]

It's not a huge leap of the imagination to Jesus, who also loves us and wants to feed us. Just as any good cook puts a lot of him or herself into a meal, so too does Jesus.

A Personal Response to the Eucharist

Our children will inevitably have their radar set to what we value. It's not hard to see this in ordinary things: the dad who's a football or baseball fan passes it on to his daughter or son; the gourmet chef teaches his or her children to appreciate fine food; the music or art lover conveys his or her enthusiasm to the kids; the Scrabble or bridge player can't wait till the children are old enough for a game. While there are always exceptions, the old adage about the apple not falling far from the tree usually holds true. The parent's priority will generally be the child's priority too. The converse is also true—most research shows it is difficult for children to become avid readers, for instance, if the habit of reading is not modeled at home.

So before we prepare our children for eucharist, we must first understand (to some extent—since a full understanding is probably impossible) what it means to us. Allow yourself ample time and, if possible, a quiet place after the kids are asleep to reflect on this section.

Look up and read one or more of the following Bible passages:

Mark 6:34-44	Mark 14:22-25
Matthew 14:13-21	Matthew 26:26-29
Luke 9:10b-17	Luke 22:14-20
John 6:1-15	1 Corinthians 11:23-26

What similarities do you find in the language describing each event? (Notice the sequence of four verbs that recur in these accounts: taking, blessing, breaking, giving.)

Reflect on these questions in the space provided.

"Jesus took bread in his hands."
How am I taken up into the hands of Jesus?

"He blessed the bread."
How am I blessed?

"... broke it"
How am I broken, wounded or changed?

"and gave it to them."
How do I give myself to others? my family? my friends?

"saying 'Take and eat, this is my body. This is my blood.'"

How do I become bread and cup for others, nurturing my friends, brothers, sisters, classmates, relatives, teachers, neighbors, even those I do not know?

In the space below, record any memories you may have of your first communion.

What has changed in your adult understanding of the eucharist? Or how is it different *now* than it was then?

Has my celebration of the eucharist become a mindless habit?

Or, what might keep me from receiving the eucharist regularly?

Which of my personal experiences with the eucharist do I most want to share with my child?

Specific Preparations for First Eucharist

Continue to read to your child as you have always done, aware of the story's power to awaken, heal, build memories and unite people. Now include some stories with eucharistic themes, such as *Old Turtle* by Douglas Wood

(Duluth, MN: Pfifer-Hamilton Publishers, 1992) or *Everybody Cooks Rice* by Norah Dooley (New York: Scholastic, 1992). You can also share an illustrated Bible story of the last supper, which children can discuss at different levels of maturity. Here is the account in language for children.

> During the meal Jesus took some bread in his hands. He blessed the bread and broke it. Then he gave it to his disciples and said, "Take this. It is my body."
>
> Jesus picked up a cup of wine and gave thanks to God. He gave it to his disciples, and they all drank some. Then he said, "This is my blood, which is poured out for many people..." (Mark 14:22-24).

You can show the similarities between meals at home and the eucharistic meal at church. Have a bread-breaking ritual at home, where each family member breaks off a piece from the same loaf and drinks from the same cup of wine or grape juice. (Explain that while this is not the eucharist, it is still a special sign that unites our family.) Continue the blessing cup ritual (p. 96), perhaps adding a prayer of anticipation or gratitude that *"Name* will soon be coming to Jesus' table."

As you are attending Mass, try to help your child identify its parts and learn the responses (p. 94). The following activities on different themes may be done as preparatory or follow-up sessions at home before or after Mass at church.

Gathering to Celebrate

Just as Jesus welcomes us to his table, so we welcome people into our homes. From an early age, children can learn the rituals of hospitality: how to greet a guest, hang up a coat, ask about others' health and concerns, help serve a snack, a beverage or a meal. If possible, teach children how to say "hello" in other languages:

> Spanish: "Hola!"
> French" "Bonjour"
> German: "Guten Tag"
> Japanese: "Konnichiwa"
> Polish: "Dzien dobry"
> Cambodian: "Sok sebai"
> Italian: "Ciao"

Also introduce your children to different ethnic foods, customs and music to reinforce the gift of cultural diversity and the meaning of the word "catholic"—universal. It is a gift to your child to teach that in Christ Jesus, we are all brothers and sisters, no matter where we live or what our ethnic or cultural background might be. When we all eat the same food and drink from the same cup in the eucharist, we are all joined to one body, the body of Christ. At his table, all are welcome.

When we gather together, we recall the baptismal symbol of the gathered assembly. You may wish to review your notes on that theme (p. 51). Do this activity with your child, showing the picture of grandmother and grandchild.

Tell a story about the *abuelita* or grandmother welcoming her grandchild.

What does she do to make the girl feel welcome? How does the girl feel?

When you enter the church, teach your child to make the sign of the cross with holy water. This reminds us of our baptism and of our identity as God's children. It is a sign that we belong to Jesus and to each other. Some parishes also sprinkle people with water in the asperges rite to remind them of their baptisms.

Liturgy of the Word: God's Stories

If you have used the section on storytelling in this book, your child will probably already be an appreciative listener. To get more out of the Sunday readings at Mass, prepare them in advance with your child; perhaps by telling the gospel story from a children's Bible or a picture book or acting it out together. You may be surprised by how much your child picks up in church when the reading is already familiar.

Or tell a few family stories. Children especially like those that feature themselves (how Sam caught the big fish, the day Alison was born, the time Gretchen took care of grandma, Carlos' first library card, etc.). Then explain that the Bible from which we read at Mass is also a collection of family stories, many of them about Jesus and his great-great-grandmas and grandpas. Children also enjoy paging through photo albums. You can point out that people in the Bible didn't have cameras, so to savor their memories, they told family stories over and over. Recall the scriptures studied in Part 1. These are the stories that shape us as a people and help us put our lives together. They bring meaning to what might otherwise be chaos.

Our experiences today continue to bring good news. Do this activity with your child.

Label a large sheet of paper "Good News." Hang it someplace visible, like your refrigerator.

Also hang a crayon, pencil or marker on a string next to it. You start: draw a picture of some good news you heard today. Ask other people in your home to fill the space by naming or drawing good news they hear. Try to fill the space in a week. Add more blank paper if you need it.

Some examples: my friend called; we had my favorite dinner; tomorrow is a holiday; we're going to a party/ the beach/a movie/a relative's house; I got new shoes.

Liturgy of the Eucharist: Gratitude for God's Gifts

Cultivate in your child an "attitude of gratitude." Remember that the word *eucharist* comes from a word meaning *thanksgiving*. You can do this in several ways:

- Choose a regular time (breakfast, dinner, bedtime) each day to voice what you are most grateful for that day.
- Create a paper chain with seven links. Have family members write or draw what they are grateful for on each link of the chain. Hang it in the kitchen or near the front door. Add to it every day to prepare for Sunday Mass.
- Invite family members to draw pictures of what they are grateful for and hang these in a visible place, such as on the refrigerator.
- Play a simplified version of Charades or Twenty Questions, in which family members mime or think of one thing they are grateful for. Others must guess what it is.
- On inexpensive, paper place mats, write the word "thanks" in large letters with crayons or permanent markers. Around the word, join your child in drawing or writing the things you are both grateful for. Then use the place mats for a special meal. (If you want them to last longer, preserve them between two sheets of clear adhesive.)

- When your child receives a gift, instill the habit of writing a thank-you note, or for younger children, drawing a picture or making a phone call to thank the giver. While this habit seems to be vanishing, the giver always welcomes an expression of gratitude.
- Make sure your children overhear parents and other trusted adults frequently voicing their appreciation. It's a contagious habit.
- Along these lines, share with children your gratitude for the unseen people who keep things running smoothly:

those who grow, sell, and prepare our food, those who keep our cities safe, those who deliver our newspapers and recycle our trash, those who maintain our hospitals, highways and schools.

Draw yourself and your family at the table with Jesus. What do you want to thank him for?

Me at the Table with Jesus

Communion: Sharing a Meal with God

We gather for eucharist to remember Jesus, responding to his request, "Do this in remembrance of me." Help your child to understand that while meals at home are like the eucharist, there is one big difference: Jesus gives *himself* as our food and drink. Whenever we eat this meal in his memory, he is here with us again. He strengthens us and gladdens us with his presence no matter how tough things may become. Do these activities with your child:

The Table at Home

We set the table at home.
Draw a circle around the plate.
Draw a line under the cup.

The Table at Church

We set the table at church.
Draw a circle around the plate.
Draw a line under the cup.

Sent Forth to Carry on Jesus' Work

The eucharist sends us forth to serve. Cultivate an attitude of service in your child from the earliest years. Preschoolers are proud of their ability to complete a chore and enjoy being praised for it. Simply feeding the dog or watering the plants makes them feel like a responsible part of the family. It also builds the conviction that they can make a difference, even in a small way. From that basis, they can go on to greater projects.

Can you tell a story about each picture?

Can you and your friends or family act out a story about these pictures?

Remember that the activities and attitudes in your home during the years between baptism and first eucharist are the child's best preparation to come to the Lord's table. Compare it to the custom in some families of separate tables for adults and children. It is a distinct "rite of passage" when a child can sit at the "grown-ups' table." But it's not all that different—learning how to handle a knife and fork, drink without spilling, eat soup without slurping and engage in courteous table conversation are the same skills needed at both tables. He or she will have a more formal preparation for first eucharist as the time approaches, but it can build only on the groundwork you have established.

Notes
1. John Tieman, "All I Will Ever Need," *America*, September 17, 1999, 20.
2. Andre Dubus, quoted in Brian Doyle, "A Graceful Man: Andre Dubus," *U.S. Catholic*, November 1999, 37.

Appendix

Family Prayers

The Doxology

Glory be to the Father
and to the Son,
and to the Holy Spirit:
as it was in the beginning,
is now
and ever shall be,
world without end. Amen.

A Child's First Prayer

Angel of God, my guardian dear,
to whom God's love commits me here,
ever this day be at my side,
to light and guard, to rule and guide.
Amen.

A Blessing

The Lord bless you and keep you;
the Lord make his face to shine upon you,
and be gracious to you;
the Lord lift up his countenance upon you,
and give you peace.

—Numbers 6:24-26

Grace before Meals

Bless us, O Lord,
and these your gifts
which we are about to receive
from your bounty.
Through Christ our Lord.
Amen.

Grace after Meals

We thank you Lord,
for these your gifts
which we have received
from your bounty.
Through Christ our Lord.
Amen.

Morning Prayer

To mark the beginning and ending of the day, you may
wish to choose different psalm verses, introducing your
family to a wide variety of them:

Awake, my soul!
Awake, O harp and lyre!
I will awake the dawn.
I will give thanks to you, O Lord,
    among the peoples;
I will sing praises to you
    among the nations.

For your steadfast love is as high as the heavens;
your faithfulness extends to the clouds.
Be exalted, O God, above the heavens.
Let your glory be over all the earth.

—Psalm 57:8-11

I call upon you, for you will answer me, O God;
incline your ear to me, hear my words.

—Psalm 17:6

Weeping may linger for the night,
but joy comes with the morning.

—Psalm 30:5

Give ear to my words, O LORD;
give heed to my sighing.
Listen to the sound of my cry,
my King and my God,
for to you I pray.

O LORD, in the morning you hear my voice;
in the morning I plead my case to you, and watch.
For you are not a God who delights in wickedness;
evil will not sojourn with you.

—Psalm 5:1-4

Night Prayer

I will both lie down and sleep in peace;
for you alone, O LORD, make me lie down in safety.

—Psalm 4:8

O LORD, my heart is not lifted up,
my eyes are not raised too high;
I do not occupy myself with things
too great and too marvelous for me.
But I have calmed and quieted my soul,
like a weaned child with its mother;
my soul is like the weaned child
that is with me.

—Psalm 131:1-2

You who live in the shelter of the Most High,
who abide in the shadow of the Almighty,
will say to the LORD,
   "My refuge and my fortress;
   my God, in whom I trust."
For God will save you from the snare of the fowler,
from the destroying pestilence.
With pinions God will cover you,
and under God's wings you shall find refuge;
God's faithfulness is a guard and a shield.

—Psalm 91:1-4

(The following two prayers may be learned one line at a time, repeated daily at a meal or at bedtime.)

The Lord's Prayer (Our Father)

Our Father, who art in heaven,
hallowed be thy name;
thy kingdom come;
thy will be done on earth as it is in heaven.
Give us this day our daily bread;
and forgive us our trespasses
as we forgive those who trespass against us;
and lead us not into temptation,
but deliver us from evil. Amen.

Hail Mary

Hail, Mary, full of grace, the Lord is with you.
Blessed are you among women,
and blessed is the fruit of your womb, Jesus.
Holy Mary, Mother of God, pray for us sinners,
now and at the hour of our death. Amen.

The Jesus Prayer

Lord Jesus Christ,
Son of God,
have mercy on me,
a sinner.

Blessing the Advent Wreath

Lord God,

let your blessing come upon us

as we light the candles of this wreath.

May the wreath and its light

be a sign of Christ's promise to bring us salvation.

May he come quickly and not delay.

We ask this through Christ our Lord.

Amen.

Taken from the National Conference of Catholic Bishops, *Book of Blessings* (New York: Catholic Book Publishing Co., 1989), #1540.

Easter Greetings

Christ is risen. Alleluia.

He is risen indeed. Alleluia.

Psalm 118:4 adapted for the Easter season:

This is the day that the LORD has made;

let us rejoice and be glad in it. Alleluia!

Books For Parents

Beginning the Journey: From Infant Baptism to First Eucharist (U.S. Catholic Conference)

Bel Geddes, Joan. *Children Praying: Why and How to Pray With Your Children* (Ave Maria)

Benson, Peter and others. *What Kids Need to Succeed* (Free Spirit)

Berg, Elizabeth. *Family Traditions: Celebrations for Holidays and Everyday* (Reader's Digest)

Coffey, Kathy. *Experiencing God with your Children* (Crossroad)

Curran, Dolores. *On Family Prayer* (Twenty-Third Publications)

Hamma, Robert. *Let's Say Grace* (Ave Maria)

Kimmel, Mary Margaret and Elizabeth Segel. *For Reading Out Loud!* (Delacorte)

Linn, Dennis, Matthew and Sheila. *Sleeping with Bread* and *Good Goats* (Paulist)

Muller, Wayne. *Sabbath* (Bantam)

Pellowski, Anne. *The Family Storytelling Handbook* (Macmillan)

Pipher, Mary. *The Shelter of Each Other* (Ballantine)

Strommen, Merton and Hardel, Richard. *Passing On the Faith* (St. Mary's)

Trelease, Jim. *The Read Aloud Handbook* (Penguin)

Books for Children

Prayer Books

A Child's Book of Celtic Prayers (Loyola)

Field, Rachel. *Prayer for a Child* (Collier Books)

Ladwig, Tim. *Psalm Twenty-Three* (African-American Family Press)

Tudor, Tasha. *Give Us This Day: The Lord's Prayer* (Philomel)

———. *The Lord Is My Shepherd: the Twenty-Third Psalm* (Philomel)

Wilkin, Eloise. *Prayers for a Small Child* (Random House)

Bible

Cousins, Lucy. *Noah's Ark* (Candlewick)

dePaola, Tomie. *Book of Bible Stories* (Putnam)

LeTord, Bijou. *Sing a New Song: A Book of Psalms* (Eerdmans)

Ray, Jane. *The Story of Creation* (Dutton)

Spier, Peter. *Noah's Ark.* (Doubleday)

Wildsmith, Brian. *The Bible Story* (Oxford University Press)

Symbols
Water

dePaola, Tomie. *Noah and the Ark* (Winston)

Getty-Sullivan, Mary Ann. *God Speaks to Us in Water Stories* (Liturgical Press)

Shulevitz, Ur. *Snow* (Farrar Straus Giroux)

Zolotow, Charlotte. *The Seashore Book* (Harper Collins)

———. *The Storm Book* (Harper Collins)

Light

Raffi, *One Light, One Sun* (Crown)

Rylant, Cynthia. *Night in the Country* (Bradbury)

Waldman, Neil and Sarah. *Light* (Harcourt Brace)

Assembly

Rylant, Cynthia. *The Relatives Came* (Bradbury)

Schenk de Regniers, Beatrice. *May I Bring a Friend?* (Atheneum)

Wells, Rosemary. *Hazel's Amazing Mother* (Dial)

Wood, Douglas. *Old Turtle* (Pfeifer-Hamilton)

Bibliography

Baker, J. Robert and others, eds. *A Baptism Sourcebook.* Chicago: Liturgy Training Publications, 1993.

Barry, William. *What Do I Want in Prayer?* New York: Paulist Press, 1994.

Beginning the Journey: From Infant Baptism to First Eucharist. Washington, DC: U.S. Catholic Conference, 1994.

Berryman, Jerome. *Godly Play.* Minneapolis: Augsburg Fortress, 1995.

Carson, Rachel. *The Sense of Wonder.* New York: Harper and Row, 1956.

Cavalletti, Sofia. *The Religious Potential of the Child.* New York: Paulist Press, 1983.

Coles, Robert. *The Spiritual Life of Children.* Boston: Houghton Mifflin, 1990.

Cooke, Bernard. *Sacraments and Sacramentality.* Mystic, CT: Twenty-Third Publications, 1985.

Covino, Paul and others. *Catechesis and Mystagogy: Infant Baptism.* Chicago and Allen, TX: Liturgy Training Publications and Tabor Publishing, 1996.

Curran, Dolores. *On Family Prayer.* Mystic, CT: Twenty-Third Publications, 1997.

Dodds, Bill. "Baptism Comes Full Circle," *Catholic Digest.* June 1999.

Doyle, Brian. "A Graceful Man: Andre Dubus." *U.S. Catholic.* November 1999.

Fagerberg, David. "Call Me by Name," *U.S. Catholic.* September 1999.

Gallagher, Maureen. *The Art of Catechesis.* New York: Paulist Press, 1998.

Grady, Thomas and Paula Huston, eds. *Signatures of Grace: Catholic Writers on the Sacraments.* New York: Dutton, 2000.

Greeley, Andrew and Mary Durkin. *How to Save the Catholic Church.* New York: Viking, 1984.

Greeley, Andrew. *The Catholic Imagination.* Berkeley: University of California Press, 2000.

————. *The Catholic Myth.* New York: Charles Scribner's Sons, 1990.

Hamma, Robert. *Landscapes of the Soul.* Notre Dame: Ave Maria Press, 1999.

Hellwig, Monika. *The Meaning of the Sacraments.* Dayton, OH: Pflaum, 1981.

Kozol, Jonathan. *Ordinary Resurrections.* New York: Crown, 2000.

Linn, Dennis, Sheila and Matthew. *Sleeping with Bread.* New York: Paulist Press, 1995.

Morris, Thomas. *The RCIA: Transforming the Church.* New York: Paulist Press, 1997.

Nelson, Gertrud Mueller. *To Dance with God.* New York: Paulist Press, 1986.

Philibert, Paul. "Landscaping the Religious Imagination," in Eleanor Bernstein and John Brooks-Leonard, eds. *Children in the Assembly of the Church.* Chicago: Liturgy Training Publications, 1992.

Pipher, Mary. *The Shelter of Each Other.* New York: Ballantine, 1996.

Rathschmidt, Jack and Gaynell B. Cronin. *Rituals for Home and Parish.* New York: Paulist Press, 1996.

Rupp, Joyce. *Dear Heart, Come Home.* New York: Crossroad, 1996.

Rylant, Cynthia. *Missing May.* New York: Orchard Books, 1992.

Sinetar, Marsha. *Spiritual Intelligence: What We Can Learn from the Early Awakening Child.* Maryknoll, NY: Orbis Books, 2000.

Tieman, John. "All I Will Ever Need," *America.* September 17, 1999.

Trokan, John and Nancy. *Families Sharing Faith: A Parents' Guide to the Grade-School Years.* New Rochelle, NY: Don Bosco Multimedia, 1992.

Tufano, Victoria, ed. *Catechesis and Mystagogy: Infant Baptism.* Chicago and Allen, TX: Liturgy Training Publications and Tabor Publishing, 1996.